SIDE by SIDE

THIRD EDITION

BOOK 3

Steven J. Molinsky
Bill Bliss

Illustrated by

Richard E. Hill

longman.com

Side by Side, 3rd edition
Student Book 3

Pearson Education, 10 Bank Street, White Plains, NY 10606

Vice president, director of publishing: *Allen Ascher*
Editorial director: *Pam Fishman*
Vice president, director of design and production: *Rhea Banker*
Director of electronic production: *Aliza Greenblatt*
Production manager: *Ray Keating*
Director of manufacturing: *Patrice Fraccio*
Digital layout specialist: *Wendy Wolf*
Associate art director: *Elizabeth Carlson*
Interior design: *Elizabeth Carlson, Wendy Wolf*
Cover design: *Elizabeth Carlson*
Copyediting: *Janet Johnston*

Contributing *Side by Side* Gazette authors: *Laura English, Meredith Westfall*

Photo credits: p. 33, (*top*) Alon Reininger/Contact Press Images Inc., (*bottom*) ©Underwood & Underwood/CORBIS; p. 34 (*top, left*) Naoki Okamoto/Black Star, (*top, center*) Michael Coyne/Black Star, (*top, right*) M. Granitsas/The Image Works, (*middle, left*) Dorothy Littell Greco/Stock Boston, (*middle, center*) Eye Ubiquitous/CORBIS, (*middle, right*) Stephen Ferry/Liaison Agency, Inc., (*bottom*) Michael Coyne/Black Star; p. 65, (*top, right*) K. H. Photo/International Stock Photography Ltd., (*upper middle, right*) Spencer Grant/PhotoEdit, (*lower middle, right*) Ken Fisher/Stone, (*bottom, left*) Carrie E. Crane, (*bottom, center*) David Young-Wolff/PhotoEdit, (*bottom, right*) Carrie E. Crane; p. 66, (*top, left*) Paul Chesley/Stone, (*top, center*) Suzanne & Nick Geary/Stone, (*top, right*) Natalie Fobes/Stone, (*middle, left*) M. Harvey/DRK Photo, (*middle, center*) Juan Carlos Ulate/Hulton/Archive, (*middle, right*) The Examiner, Mark Costantini/AP/Wide World Photos, (*bottom*) Michael Newman/PhotoEdit; p.111, (*top*) Eric Risberg/AP/Wide World Photos, (*bottom, left*) ©The Walt Disney Company. All Rights Reserved./The Neal Peters Collection, (*bottom, right*) Mike Blake/Reuters/Liaison Agency, Inc.; p. 112, (*top, left*) ©Paul A. Souders/CORBIS, (*top, center*) Charles Gupton/Stock Boston, (*top, right*) Richard Lord/PhotoEdit, (*middle, left*) ©David & Peter Turnley/CORBIS, (*middle, center*) David Young-Wolff/PhotoEdit, (*middle, right*) Yann Arthus-Bertrand/CORBIS, (*bottom*) Frank Siteman/Stock Boston; p. 145, Rhoda Sidney/Stock Boston; p. 146, (*row 1, far left*) John Terence Turner/FPG International LLC, (*row 1, second from left*) T. Zuidema/The Image Works, (*row 1, second from right*) John Eastcott/Yva Momatiuk/Stock Boston,(*row 1, far right*) John Elk III/Stock Boston, (*row 2, far left*) Caroline Penn/CORBIS, (*row 2, second from left*) John Eastcott/Yva Momatiuk/Woodfin Camp & Associates, (*row 2, second from right*) VCG/FPG International LLC, (*row 2, far right*) SuperStock, Inc., (*row 3, center*) Alan Oddie/PhotoEdit, (*row 4, far left*) Jonathan Blair/CORBIS, (*row 4, second from left*) Spencer Grant/PhotoEdit, (*row 4, center*) Talby/CORBIS, (*row 4, second from right*) Fujifotos/The Image Works, (*row 4, far right*) Elyse Lewin/The Image Bank; p. 147, (*top, left*) Gary Buss/FPG International LLC, (*top, center*) Richard Lord/The Image Works, (*top, right*) Robert Fried/Stock Boston, (*bottom, far left*) SuperStock, Inc., (*bottom, second from left*) Gary A. Conner/PhotoEdit, (*bottom, second from right*) Myrleen Cate/PhotoEdit, (*bottom, far right*) Rhoda Sidney/Stock Boston.

The authors gratefully acknowledge the contribution
of Tina Carver in the development of the original
Side by Side program.

ISBN 0-13-026874-7   (Regular Edition)

10 – RRD – 07

ISBN 0-13-184179-3   (Student Book with Audio Highlights)

4 5 6 7 8 9 10 – RRD – 07

ISBN 0-13-183936-5   (International Edition)

7 8 9 10 – RRD – 07

Printed in the United States of America

CONTENTS

How to Say It! (Communication Strategies)

Pronunciation

Review:
Simple Present Tense
Present Continuous Tense

Subject & Object Pronouns
Possessive Adjectives
Time Expressions

- **Describing Habitual and Ongoing Activities**
- **Telling About Likes and Dislikes**

- **Describing Frequency of Actions**
- **Telling About Personal Background and Interests**

VOCABULARY PREVIEW

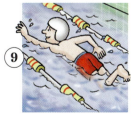

1. actor	**5.** player	**9.** swimmer
2. dancer	**6.** singer	**10.** teacher
3. driver	**7.** skater	**11.** typist
4. instructor	**8.** skier	**12.** violinist

They're Busy

Am	I		
Is	he / she / it	eating?	
Are	we / you / they		

Yes,	I	am.
	he / she / it	is.
	we / you / they	are.

(I am)	I'm	
(He is)	He's	
(She is)	She's	
(It is)	It's	eating.
(We are)	We're	
(You are)	You're	
(They are)	They're	

A. Are you busy?

B. Yes, I am. I'm studying.

A. What are you studying?

B. I'm studying English.

1. Is Alan busy?
baking • cookies

2. Is Doris busy?
reading • the newspaper

3. Are your parents busy?
painting • the kitchen

4. Are you busy?
writing • a letter

5. Are you and Tom busy?
cooking • dinner

6. Is Ann busy?
knitting • a sweater

7. Is your brother busy?
ironing • his shirts

8. Are Mr. and Mrs. Garcia busy?
cleaning • their garage

9. Is Beethoven busy?
composing • a symphony

What Are They Doing?

| Do | I / we / you / they | eat? |
| Does | he / she / it | |

| Yes, | I / we / you / they | do. |
| | he / she / it | does. |

| I / We / You / They | eat. |
| He / She / It | eats. |

A. What are you doing?

B. I'm practicing the piano.

A. Do you practice the piano very often?

B. Yes, I do. I practice the piano whenever I can.

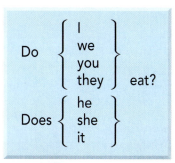

1. What's Carol doing?
watch the news

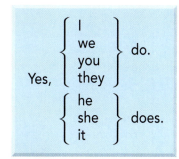

2. What's Edward doing?
swim

3. What are you doing?
study math

4. What are Mr. and Mrs. Park doing?
exercise

5. What are you and your friend doing?
play Scrabble

6. What's Mrs. Anderson doing?
read poetry

7. What's Daniel doing?
play baseball with his daughter

8. What are you doing?
chat online with my friends

9.

3

Do You Like to Ski?

No,	I / we / you / they	don't. (do not)
	he / she / it	doesn't. (does not)

I'm not . . .

He / She / It	isn't . . . (is not)
We / You / They	aren't . . . (are not)

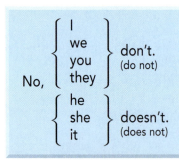

A. Do you like to ski?

B. No, I don't. I'm not a very good skier.

1. Does Richard like to sing?
singer

2. Does Brenda like to swim?
swimmer

3. Do Mr. and Mrs. Adams like to skate?
skaters

4. Does Arthur like to dance?
dancer

5. Do you like to type?
typist

6. Do you and your friend like to act?
actors

7. Does your grandmother like to drive?
driver

8. Do you like to play sports?
athlete

9. Does Howard like to cook?
cook

PRACTICING

My sisters, my brother, and I are busy this afternoon. We're staying after school, and we're practicing different things.

I'm practicing soccer. I practice soccer every day after school. My soccer coach tells me I'm an excellent soccer player, and my friends tell me I play soccer better than anyone else in the school. I want to be a professional soccer player when I grow up. That's why I practice every day.

My sister Anita is practicing tennis. She practices tennis every day after school. Her tennis coach tells her she's an excellent tennis player, and her friends tell her she plays tennis better than anyone else in the school. Anita wants to be a professional tennis player when she grows up. That's why she practices every day.

My brother Hector is practicing the violin. He practices the violin every day after school. His music teacher tells him he's an excellent violinist, and his friends tell him he plays the violin better than anyone else in the school. Hector wants to be a professional violinist when he grows up. That's why he practices every day.

My sisters Jenny and Vanessa are practicing ballet. They practice ballet every day after school. Their ballet instructor tells them they're excellent ballet dancers, and their friends tell them they dance better than anyone else in the school. Jenny and Vanessa want to be professional ballet dancers when they grow up. That's why they practice every day.

✔️ READING CHECK-UP

Q & A

You're talking with the person who told the story on page 5. Using this model, create dialogs based on the story.

A. *What's your sister Anita* doing?
B. *She's* practicing *tennis*.
A. *Does she* practice very often?
B. Yes, *she does*. *She practices* every day after school.
A. *Is she a* good *tennis player*?
B. Yes, *she is*. *Her tennis instructor* says *she's* excellent, and *her* friends tell *her she plays tennis* better than anyone else in the school.

LISTENING

Listen and choose the correct answer.

1. a. I practice football.
   b. I'm practicing football.

2. a. Yes, I am.
   b. Yes, I do.

3. a. Yes, I am.
   b. Yes, I do.

4. a. She reads the newspaper.
   b. She's reading the newspaper.

5. a. My husband cooks.
   b. My husband is cooking.

6. a. No, they aren't.
   b. No, they don't.

7. a. Yes, when he grows up.
   b. Yes, when she grows up.

8. a. Yes, we do.
   b. Yes, you do.

9. a. Yes, they are.
   b. Yes, we are.

10. a. He's playing soccer.
    b. He wants to be a soccer player.

IN YOUR OWN WORDS

FOR WRITING AND DISCUSSION

Tell about studying English.

Do you go to English class? Where?
When do you go to class?
What's your teacher's name?

When do you practice English?
How do you practice?
Who do you practice with?

🔴 6

How Often?

I	my	me
he	his	him
she	her	her
it	its	it
we	our	us
you	your	you
they	their	them

Time Expressions

every day/week/weekend/month/year
every morning/afternoon/evening/night
every Sunday/Monday/Tuesday/. . .
every Sunday morning/afternoon/evening/night
every January/February/March/. . .

once a
twice a   day/week/month/year
three times a

all the time

A. Who are you calling?

B. **I'm** calling **my** sister in San Francisco.

A. How often do you call **her**?

B. I call **her** every Sunday evening.

A. What are George and Herman talking about?

B. **They're** talking about **their** grandchildren.

A. How often do they talk about **them**?

B. They talk about **them** all the time.

1. Who is Mr. Tanaka calling?
son in New York

2. Who is Mrs. Kramer writing to?
daughter in the army

3. What are the students talking about?
teachers

4. Who is Lenny arguing with?
landlord

5. Who is Martha sending an e-mail to?
granddaughter in Orlando

6. Who is Mr. Crabapple shouting at?
employees

7. What are your parents complaining about?
telephone bill

8. What is George watching?
favorite TV talk show

9. Who is Little Red Riding Hood visiting?
grandmother

10.

How to Say It!

Asking for and Reacting to Information

A. Tell me, *where are you from?*

B. *I'm from Madagascar.*

A. { Oh.
Really?
Oh, really?
That's interesting.

Practice the interactions on this page, using expressions for asking for and reacting to information.

INTERACTIONS *Sharing Opinions*

Talking about yourself:

> Where are you from?
> Where do you live now?

> What do you do?
> Where do you work / study?

Talking about family:

> Are you married?
> Are you single?

> Who are the people in your family?*
> What are their names?
> Where do they live?

Talking about interests:

> What do you like to do
> in your free time?

> How often do you watch TV?
> listen to music? go to movies?
> play sports?

Practice conversations with other students. Get to know each other as you talk about yourselves, your families, and your interests.

* wife, husband, mother, father, daughter, son, sister, brother, grandmother, grandfather, granddaughter, grandson, aunt, uncle, cousin

Write in your journal about yourself, your family, and your interests.

9

Listen. Then say it.

Who are you calling?

What are they talking about?

Where are you from?

What are you doing?

Say it. Then listen.

Who are you writing to?

What are they complaining about?

Where are they studying?

What are their names?

CHAPTER SUMMARY

GRAMMAR

PRESENT CONTINUOUS TENSE

(I am)	I'm	
(He is)	He's	
(She is)	She's	eating.
(It is)	It's	
(We are)	We're	
(You are)	You're	
(They are)	They're	

Am	I	
Is	he / she / it	eating?
Are	we / you / they	

TO BE: SHORT ANSWERS

Yes,	I	am.
	he / she / it	is.
	we / you / they	are.

No,	I'm	not.
	he / she / it	isn't.
	we / you / they	aren't.

SIMPLE PRESENT TENSE

I / We / You / They	eat.
He / She / It	eats.

Do	I / we / you / they	eat?
Does	he / she / it	

Yes,	I / we / you / they	do.
	he / she / it	does.

No,	I / we / you / they	don't.
	he / she / it	doesn't.

Subject Pronouns	Possessive Adjectives	Object Pronouns
I	my	me
he	his	him
she	her	her
it	its	it
we	our	us
you	your	you
they	their	them

KEY VOCABULARY

ACTIONS

act, argue, bake, call, chat, clean, complain, compose, cook, dance, do, drive, exercise, go, iron, knit, live, paint, play, practice, read, send, shout, sing, skate, ski, study, swim, talk, type, visit, watch, work, write

AGENT NOUNS

actor, dancer, driver, instructor, player, singer, skater, skier, swimmer, teacher, typist, violinist

FAMILY MEMBERS

brother, daughter, father, grandchildren, granddaughter, grandfather, grandmother, grandson, husband, mother, parents, sister, son, wife

2

Review:
Simple Past Tense (Regular and Irregular Verbs)
Past Continuous Tense

- **Reporting Past Activities**
- **Mishaps**
- **Difficult Experiences**
- **Describing a Trip**

VOCABULARY PREVIEW

1. break – broke
2. buy – bought
3. cut – cut
4. eat – ate
5. fall – fell

6. go – went
7. hurt – hurt
8. lose – lost
9. meet – met
10. ride – rode

11. sing – sang
12. speak – spoke
13. swim – swam
14. teach – taught
15. write – wrote

Did They Sleep Well Last Night?

What did
{
I
he
she
it
we
you
they
}
do?

I
He
She
It
We
You
They
}
worked.

I
He
She
It
}
was
tired.
We
You
They
}
were

A. Did Emma sleep well last night?

B. Yes, she did. She was VERY tired.

A. Why? What did she do yesterday?

B. She worked in her garden all day.

1. *you*
study English

2. *Rick*
paint his apartment

3. *you and your brother*
wash windows

4. *Ms. Taylor*
teach

5. *Henry*
deliver pizzas

6. *Sarah*
write letters

7. *Matthew*
ride his bicycle

8. *the president*
meet important people

9.

Did Robert Shout at His Dog?

Yes / No, { I he she it we you they } did / didn't.
(did not)

{ I He She It } was / wasn't . . .
(was not)

{ We You They } were / weren't . . .
(were not)

A. Did Robert shout at his dog?

B. Yes, he did. He was angry.

A. Did Helen sleep well last night?

B. No, she didn't. She wasn't tired.

1. Did Howard fall asleep in class?
Yes, _____. _____ bored.

2. Did Amy take the plane to Rio?
No, _____. _____ on time.

3. Did you cry during the movie?
Yes, _____. _____ sad.

4. Did Brad do well on his exam?
No, _____. _____ prepared.

5. Did Frank and James forget their lines during the school play?
Yes, _____. _____ nervous.

6. Did you and your sister cover your eyes during the science fiction movie?
No, _____. _____ scared.

7. Did Abby finish her dinner?
Yes, _____. _____ hungry.

8. Did Timmy drink all his milk?
No, _____. _____ thirsty.

13

How Did Marty Break His Leg?

I		
He	was	
She		working.
It		
We		
You	were	
They		

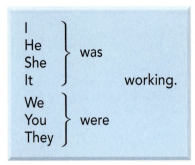

A. How did Marty break his leg?

B. He broke it while he was snowboarding.

A. That's too bad!

1. How did Greta sprain her ankle?
play volleyball

2. How did Larry lose his wallet?
hike in the woods

3. How did Brian cut himself?
shave

4. How did Mr. and Mrs. Harper burn themselves?
prepare dinner

5. How did Stella rip her pants?
do her daily exercises

6. How did your grandfather trip and fall?
get off a bus

7. How did Peter poke himself in the eye?
talk on his cell phone

8. How did Marilyn cut herself?
chop onions

9. How did Timothy get a black eye?
fight with the kid across the street

10. How did Presto the Magician hurt himself?
practice a new magic trick

How to Say It!

Reacting to Bad News

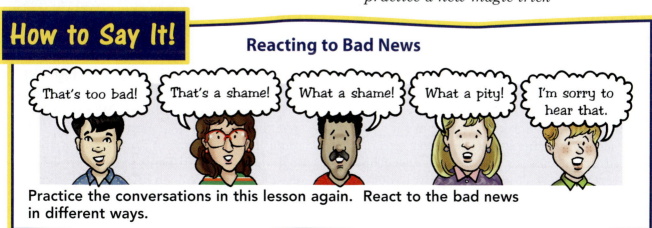

That's too bad!

That's a shame!

What a shame!

What a pity!

I'm sorry to hear that.

Practice the conversations in this lesson again. React to the bad news in different ways.

DIFFICULT EXPERIENCES

Ms. Henderson usually teaches very well, but she didn't teach very well this morning. In fact, she taught very badly. While she was teaching, the school principal was sitting at the back of the room and watching her. It was a very difficult experience for Ms. Henderson. She realized she wasn't teaching very well, but she couldn't do anything about it. She was too nervous.

Stuart usually types very well, but he didn't type very well today. In fact, he typed very badly. While he was typing, his supervisor was standing behind him and looking over his shoulder. It was a difficult experience for Stuart. He realized he wasn't typing very well, but he couldn't do anything about it. He was too upset.

The Baxter Boys usually sing very well, but they didn't sing very well last night. In fact, they sang very badly. While they were singing, their parents were sitting in the audience and waving at them. It was a difficult experience for the Baxter Boys. They realized they weren't singing very well, but they couldn't do anything about it. They were too embarrassed.

The president usually speaks very well, but he didn't speak very well this afternoon. In fact, he spoke very badly. While he was speaking, several demonstrators were standing at the back of the room and shouting at him. It was a difficult experience for the president. He realized he wasn't speaking very well, but he couldn't do anything about it. He was too angry.

✔️ READING *CHECK-UP*

Q & A

Ms. Henderson, Stuart, the Baxter Boys, and the president are talking with friends about their difficult experiences. Using this model, create dialogs based on the story on page 16.

A. You know . . . I didn't *teach* very well *this morning*.
B. You didn't?
A. No. In fact, I *taught* very badly.
B. That's strange. You usually *teach* VERY well. What happened?
A. While I was *teaching, the school principal was sitting at the back of the room and watching me.*
B. Oh. I bet that was a very difficult experience for you.
A. It was. I *was* very *nervous*.

MATCH

We often use colorful expressions to describe how we feel. Try to match the following expressions with the feelings they describe.

____ **1.** "My stomach is growling."
____ **2.** "I can't keep my eyes open."
____ **3.** "I'm jumping for joy!"
____ **4.** "I'm seeing red!"
____ **5.** "I'm feeling blue."
____ **6.** "I'm on pins and needles!"
____ **7.** "I'm shaking like a leaf!"
____ **8.** "I'm ashamed to look at them straight in the eye."

   a. angry
   b. embarrassed
   c. tired
   d. nervous
   e. scared
   f. hungry
   g. sad
   h. happy

How About You?

Tell about a difficult experience you had. What happened? How did you feel?

LISTENING

Listen and choose the correct answer.

1. a. Yes, I did.
   b. Yes, I was.

2. a. Yes, they did.
   b. Yes, they were.

3. a. He played soccer.
   b. He was playing soccer.

4. a. No. I wasn't hungry.
   b. Yes. I wasn't hungry.

5. a. He lost his wallet.
   b. He was jogging in the park.

6. a. She was nervous.
   b. She was looking over my shoulder.

7. a. Yes. I was prepared.
   b. No. I was prepared.

8. a. I cut myself.
   b. I was too upset.

Tell Me About Your Vacation

Tell me about your vacation.

It was very nice.

1. **A.** Did you go to Paris?
   B. No, __we didn't__ .
   A. Where _____ did you go _____?
   B. _____ We went _____ to Rome.

2. **A.** Did you get there by boat?
   B. No, _____.
   A. How _____?
   B. _____ by plane.

3. **A.** Did you stay in a big hotel?
   B. No, _____.
   A. What kind of _____?
   B. _____ a small hotel.

4. **A.** Did you eat in fancy restaurants?
   B. No, _____.
   A. Where _____?
   B. _____ cheap restaurants.

Where is the post office?

5. **A.** Did you speak Italian?
   B. No, _____.
   A. What language _____?
   B. _____ English.

6. **A.** Did you take many pictures?
   B. No, _____.
   A. How many _____?
   B. _____ just a few pictures.

18

7. A. Did you buy any clothing?

B. No, _____.

A. What _____?

B. _____ souvenirs.

8. A. Did you swim in the Mediterranean?

B. No, _____.

A. Where _____?

B. _____ in the pool at our hotel.

9. A. Did you see the Colosseum?

B. No, _____.

A. What _____?

B. _____ the Vatican.

10. A. Did you get around the city by taxi?

B. No, _____.

A. How _____?

B. _____ by bus.

11. A. Did you meet a lot of Italians?

B. No, _____.

A. Who _____?

B. _____ a lot of other tourists.

12. A. Did you come home by plane?

B. No, _____.

A. How _____?

B. _____ by boat.

SIDE *by* SIDE JOURNAL

Write in your journal about a trip you took. Where did you go? How did you get there? Where did you stay? What did you do there? How long were you there? Did you have a good time?

(If you have some photographs of your trip, bring them to class and talk about them with other students.)

Listen. Then say it.	Say it. Then listen.
Did you go to Madrid?	Did you meet a lot of people?
Did you speak Spanish?	Did you have a good time?
Where did you stay?	How did you get there?
What did you do?	When did you get home?

CHAPTER SUMMARY

GRAMMAR

SIMPLE PAST TENSE

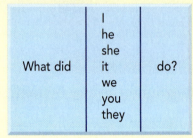

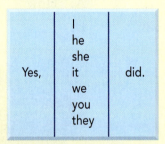

PAST CONTINUOUS TENSE

I / He / She / It	was	working.
We / You / They	were	

KEY VOCABULARY

REGULAR VERBS

burn	jump	rip	talk
chop	look	shave	trip
cover	paint	shout	type
cry	play	snowboard	wash
deliver	poke	sprain	watch
finish	practice	stay	wave
growl	prepare	study	work
hike	realize		

IRREGULAR VERBS

break – broke	feel – felt	lose – lost	speak – spoke
buy – bought	fight – fought	meet – met	stand – stood
come – came	forget – forgot	ride – rode	swim – swam
cut – cut	get – got	see – saw	take – took
do – did	go – went	shake – shook	teach – taught
drink – drank	have – had	sing – sang	tell – told
eat – ate	hurt – hurt	sit – sat	write – wrote
fall – fell	keep – kept	sleep – slept	

20

3

Review:
Future: Going to
Future: Will
Future Continuous Tense

Time Expressions
Possessive Pronouns

- **Describing Future Plans and Intentions**
- **Telling About the Future**
- **Expressing Time and Duration**

- **Talking on the Telephone**
- **Plans for the Future**
- **Asking a Favor**

VOCABULARY PREVIEW

yesterday   *today*   *tomorrow*

1. yesterday morning	4. yesterday afternoon	7. yesterday evening	10. last night
2. this morning	5. this afternoon	8. this evening	11. tonight
3. tomorrow morning	6. tomorrow afternoon	9. tomorrow evening	12. tomorrow night

What Are They Going to Do?

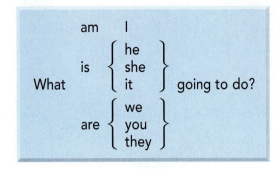

	am	I		
What	is	he / she / it	going to do?	
	are	we / you / they		

(I am)	I'm	
(He is)	He's	
(She is)	She's	
(It is)	It's	going to read.
(We are)	We're	
(You are)	You're	
(They are)	They're	

Time Expressions

yesterday / this / tomorrow	morning / afternoon / evening	last night / tonight / tomorrow night

last / this / next	week / month / year / Sunday / Monday / . . .
	spring / summer / . . .
	January / February / . . .

A. Are you going to buy a donut this morning?

B. No, I'm not. I bought a donut YESTERDAY morning.

A. What are you going to buy?

B. I'm going to buy a muffin.

1. Is Mr. Hopper going to have cake for dessert tonight?

   ice cream

2. Is Valerie going to sing folk songs this evening?

   Broadway show tunes

3. Are you and your family going to go to Europe this summer?

   Hawaii

4. Is Gary going to wear his gray suit today?

   his blue suit

5. Are your parents going to watch the movie on Channel 4 this Friday night?

   the news program on Channel 7

6. Is Elizabeth going to go out with Jonathan this Saturday evening?

   Bob

7. Is the chef going to make onion soup today?

   pea soup

8. Is your sister going to take biology this semester?

   astronomy

9. Are you and your brother going to play cards this afternoon?

   chess

10. Are you going to be Superman this Halloween?

    Batman

READING

PLANS FOR THE WEEKEND

It's Friday afternoon, and all the employees at the Liberty Insurance Company are thinking about their plans for the weekend. Milton is going to work in his garden. Diane is going to go hiking in the mountains. Carmen and Tom are going to play tennis. Jack is going to go water-skiing. Kate is going to build a tree house for her children. And Ray and his family are going to have a picnic.

Unfortunately, the employees at the Liberty Insurance Company are going to be very disappointed. According to the radio, it's going to "rain cats and dogs" all weekend.

 ## READING *CHECK-UP*

Q & A

The employees at the Liberty Insurance Company are talking with each other. Using this model, create dialogs based on the story.

A. Tell me, *Milton*, what are you going to do this weekend?
B. I'm going to *work in my garden*. How about you, *Diane*? What are YOU going to do?
A. I'm going to *go hiking in the mountains*.
B. Well, have a nice weekend.
A. You, too.

How About You?

What are you going to do this weekend? What's the weather forecast?

LISTENING

Listen to the conversation and choose the answer that is true.

1. a. He's going to wear his gray suit.
   b. He's going to wear his brown suit.

2. a. They're going to have dinner at home.
   b. They're going to have dinner at a restaurant.

3. a. They're going to watch Channel 5.
   b. They're going to watch Channel 9.

4. a. He's going to call a mechanic.
   b. He's going to call an electrician.

5. a. She's going to go to the supermarket tomorrow.
   b. She's going to work in her garden tomorrow.

6. a. They're going to buy the computer.
   b. They aren't going to buy the computer.

Will Ms. Martinez Return Soon?

(I will)	I'll	
(He will)	He'll	
(She will)	She'll	
(It will)	It'll	work.
(We will)	We'll	
(You will)	You'll	
(They will)	They'll	

I	
He	
She	
It	won't work.
We	(will not)
You	
They	

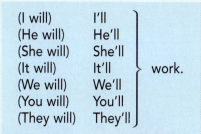

A. Will Ms. Martinez return soon?

B. Yes, she will. She'll return in a little while.

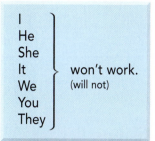

A. Will your sister return soon?

B. No, she won't. She won't return for a long time.

1. Will the play begin soon?

Yes, _____. _____ at 7:30.

2. Will the concert begin soon?

No, _____. _____ until 8:00.

3. Will Ken and Kim see each other again soon?

Yes, _____. _____ this Saturday night.

4. Will Larry and Lisa see each other again soon?

No, _____. _____ until next year.

5. Will the train arrive soon?

Yes, _____. _____ in a few minutes.

6. Will Flight 216 arrive soon?

No, _____. _____ for several hours.

7. Will David get out of the hospital soon?

Yes, _____. _____ in a few days.

8. Will Ralph get out of jail soon?

No, _____. _____ for a few years.

Will You Be Home This Evening?

| I'll
He'll
She'll
It'll
We'll
You'll
They'll | be working. |

A. Will you be home this evening?

B. Yes, I will. I'll be **watching videos**.

A. Will Nancy be home this evening?

B. No, she won't. She'll be **working overtime**.

1. *you*
   pay bills

2. *Angela*
   shop at the mall

3. *Mr. and Mrs. Chen*
   paint their kitchen

4. *your sister*
   attend a meeting

5. *you and your family*
   ice skate

6. *Vincent*
   browse the web

7. *you*
   do research at the
   library

8. *Tess*
   fill out her income tax
   form

9. *Mr. and Mrs. Silva*
   work out at their health
   club

Can You Call Back a Little Later?

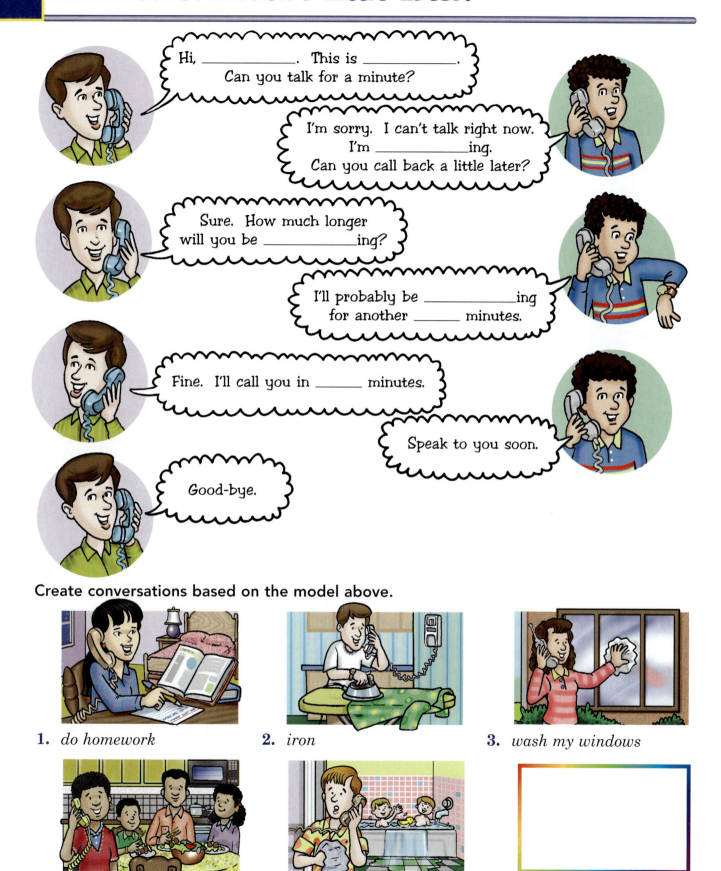

Hi, _____. This is _____. Can you talk for a minute?

I'm sorry. I can't talk right now. I'm _____ing. Can you call back a little later?

Sure. How much longer will you be _____ing?

I'll probably be _____ing for another _____ minutes.

Fine. I'll call you in _____ minutes.

Speak to you soon.

Good-bye.

Create conversations based on the model above.

1. *do homework*

2. *iron*

3. *wash my windows*

4. *have dinner*

5. *give the kids a bath*

6.

Could You Do Me a Favor?

I	me	mine
he	him	his
she	her	hers
it	it	—
we	us	ours
you	you	yours
they	them	theirs

Joe

A. Could you do me a favor?

B. Sure. What is it?

A. I have to fix a flat tire, and I don't have a jack. Could I possibly borrow yours?

B. I'm sorry. I'm afraid I don't have one.

A. Oh. Do you know anybody who does?

B. Yes. You should call Joe. I'm sure he'll be happy to lend you his.

A. Thanks. I'll call him right away.

A. Could you do me a favor?

B. Sure. What is it?

A. I have to _____, and I don't have a _____. Could I possibly borrow yours?

B. I'm sorry. I'm afraid I don't have one.

A. Oh. Do you know anybody who does?

B. Yes. You should call _____. I'm sure _____'ll be happy to lend you _____ (his / hers / theirs).

A. Thanks. I'll call _____ (him / her / them) right away.

1. *fix my front steps*
hammer

2. *assemble my new*
bookshelf
screwdriver

3. *write a composition*
dictionary

4. *adjust my satellite dish*
ladder

5. *go to a wedding*
tuxedo

6.

How to Say It!

Asking for a Favor

A.
{
Could you do me a favor?
Could you possibly do me a favor?
Could you do a favor for me?
Could I ask you a favor?
}

B. Sure. What is it?

Practice the conversations in this lesson again. Ask for a favor in different ways.

SAYING GOOD-BYE

Mr. and Mrs. Karpov are at the Moscow airport. They're saying good-bye to their son Sasha and his family. It's a very emotional day. In a few minutes, Sasha and his family will get on a plane and fly to Canada. They won't be coming back. They're leaving Russia permanently, and Mr. and Mrs. Karpov won't be seeing them for a long, long time.

Sasha and his family are excited about their plans for the future. They're going to stay with his wife's relatives in Toronto. Sasha will work in the family's restaurant. His wife, Marina, will take any job she can find during the day, and she'll study English at night. The children will begin school in September.

Mr. and Mrs. Karpov are both happy and sad. They're happy because they know that their son will have a good life in his new home. However, they're sad because they know they're going to be very lonely. Their apartment will be quiet and empty, and they won't see their grandchildren grow up.

Some day Mr. and Mrs. Karpov will visit Toronto, or perhaps they'll even move there. But until then, they're going to miss their family very much. As you can imagine, it's very difficult for them to say good-bye.

✔ READING CHECK-UP

TRUE OR FALSE?

1. Sasha and his family will be leaving Russia for a few minutes.
2. Marina's relatives live in Toronto.
3. Mr. Karpov is happy, and Mrs. Karpov is sad.
4. Mr. and Mrs. Karpov might move to Toronto.
5. Mr. and Mrs. Karpov are sad because they'll be at the Moscow airport until they visit Toronto or move there.

How About You?

- Tell about an emotional day in your life when you had to say good-bye.

- Tell about YOUR plans for the future.

Jerry is looking forward to this weekend. He isn't going to think about work. He's going to read a few magazines, work on his car, and relax at home with his family.

Amanda is looking forward to her birthday. Her sister is going to have a party for her, and all her co-workers and friends are going to be there.

Mr. and Mrs. Cook are looking forward to their summer vacation. They're going to go camping. They're going to hike several miles every day, take a lot of pictures, and forget about all their problems at home.

Mr. and Mrs. Lee are looking forward to their retirement. They're going to get up late every morning, visit friends every afternoon, and enjoy quiet evenings at home together.

What are YOU looking forward to? A birthday? a holiday? a day off? Talk about it with other students in your class.

Write in your journal about something you're looking forward to: What are you looking forward to? When is it going to happen? What are you going to do?

going to = gonna

Listen. Then say it.

Are you going to buy bread today?

What are you going to eat?

I'm going to go camping.

Say it. Then listen.

Is she going to watch TV?

What's he going to wear?

They're going to make dinner.

CHAPTER SUMMARY

GRAMMAR

FUTURE: GOING TO

	am	I	
What	is	he she it	going to do?
	are	we you they	

(I am)	I'm	
(He is)	He's	
(She is)	She's	
(It is)	It's	going to read.
(We are)	We're	
(You are)	You're	
(They are)	They're	

POSSESSIVE PRONOUNS

mine
his
hers
—
ours
yours
theirs

FUTURE: WILL

(I will)	I'll	
(He will)	He'll	
(She will)	She'll	
(It will)	It'll	work.
(We will)	We'll	
(You will)	You'll	
(They will)	They'll	

I	
He	
She	
It	won't work.
We	
You	
They	

FUTURE CONTINUOUS TENSE

(I will)	I'll	
(He will)	He'll	
(She will)	She'll	
(It will)	It'll	be working.
(We will)	We'll	
(You will)	You'll	
(They will)	They'll	

KEY VOCABULARY

ACTIONS AND ACTIVITIES

adjust	call	get	happen	make	say	visit
arrive	call back	get out	have	miss	see	wash
ask	come back	get up	hike	move	shop	watch
assemble	do homework	give	ice skate	paint	sing	wear
attend	do research	go	imagine	pay bills	speak	work
be	enjoy	go camping	iron	play	stay	work on
begin	fill out	go hiking	know	rain	study	work out
borrow	find	go out with	leave	read	take	write
browse	fix	go water-skiing	lend	relax	talk	
build	fly	grow up	look forward to	return	think	
buy	forget					

Feature Article
Fact File
Around the World
Interview
We've Got Mail!

Global Exchange
Listening
Fun with Idioms
What Are They
Saying?

Volume 3   Number 1

Immigration Around the World

Where do immigrants move, and why?

More than 145 million immigrants live outside their native countries. Immigrants move to other countries for different reasons. Some people move because of war, political or economic problems, or natural disasters such as earthquakes and floods. Some immigrants move to be with family members, to marry, or to find better living conditions.

Where are immigrants moving from? And what countries are they moving to? One of the largest immigration flows is from Latin America and Asia to the United States. Another immigrant flow is from Eastern Europe, the former Soviet republics, and North Africa to Western Europe. Many immigrants also move from Africa and Asia to the Middle East. In countries such as Saudi Arabia, 90% of the total population is now foreign born.

When immigrants arrive in a new country, they often live in urban neighborhoods. As a result of immigration, many city neighborhoods change. Immigrants open new stores, restaurants, and other businesses. For example, the historic Esquilino neighborhood in Rome is now the home of a large number of Chinese immigrants. There are also

Immigrants arriving in their new country

many new immigrants from Albania, Moldova, Bulgaria, and Ukraine. In some schools in Athens, 50% of the children are foreign born. Los Angeles and New York are two cities in the United States with very large immigrant populations. In Los Angeles, 37% of the population is foreign born, and children in the public schools speak 82 different languages. In New York, 40% of the population is foreign born, and children speak 140 different languages in the schools.

Ellis Island

Ellis Island was an immigration center on an island in the harbor of New York City. Between 1892 and 1954, 12 million immigrants passed through Ellis Island. At Ellis Island, immigration officials checked immigrants' documents, gave them medical examinations, and decided if the immigrants could stay in the United States. Most

Ellis Island registration hall

immigrants came from Italy, Russia, Hungary, Austria, Austria-Hungary, Germany, England, and Ireland. More than 40% of all Americans today have a present or past relative who came through Ellis Island.

FACT FILE

Countries with Large Numbers of Immigrants

COUNTRY	IMMIGRANT POPULATION (IN MILLIONS)
United States	28.4
Germany	7.5
Saudi Arabia	6
Canada	4.9
Australia	4.4
France	4.3

AROUND THE WORLD

Immigrant Neighborhoods

There are many interesting immigrant neighborhoods around the world. In these neighborhoods, immigrants can often speak their native languages, buy products from their countries, and eat in restaurants that serve their favorite foods.

a Cuban neighborhood in Miami, Florida

Vietnamese immigrants in Sydney, Australia

Turkish immigrants in Berlin, Germany

Chinatown in Toronto, Canada

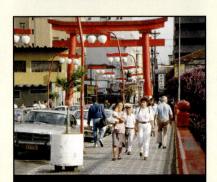

Japanese immigrants in Sao Paulo, Brazil

a Russian neighborhood in Brooklyn, New York

What are different immigrant neighborhoods you know?

Interview

A Side by Side Gazette reporter recently visited Mr. Tran Nguyen, a Vietnamese immigrant in Australia. Mr. Nguyen lives and works in a Vietnamese and Chinese neighborhood in the suburbs of Melbourne.

Q: When did you immigrate to Australia, and why?

A: Well, my brother left Vietnam in 1983 and came here to Australia. Seven years later, his wife and children joined him. I came here three years ago with my wife and children to be with my brother and his family.

Q: Do you work?

A: Yes. I work seven days a week in my brother's restaurant, and I go to English classes at night.

Q: What did you do in Vietnam?

A: I was a teacher. I taught mathematics. I want to be a teacher here someday, but first I want to send my children to college.

Q: What do you miss most about Vietnam?

A: I miss my community and my friends. In Vietnam, people took care of each other. It's not the same here. Everyone here works very hard. People are very busy. They don't have much time to spend with friends.

Q: What do you like about your life here?

A: We have many opportunities. My wife and I both have good jobs, and my son and daughter will go to college someday. I think we will have a very good future here, and we're very grateful.

We've Got Mail!

Dear Side by Side,

I have a question about tenses in English. Sometimes I hear people use the present tense when they are talking about the future. For example, I was watching a TV program in English yesterday, and I heard a man say, "I'm flying to London tomorrow. My plane leaves at 9:30." But if a man is talking about tomorrow, shouldn't he use the future tense? I think the correct way to say this is: "I'm going to fly to London tomorrow. My plane will leave at 9:30." Did the man on the TV program make a mistake?

Sincerely,

"Tense About the Future"

Dear "Tense About the Future,"

Your question is a very good one. No, the man on the TV program didn't make a mistake. We often use the present tense to talk about events in the future or about definite plans that we have. For example, you can say:

My brother's wedding is next Saturday.
I'm having a party tomorrow.
They're going to the beach this weekend.
The plumber is coming tomorrow morning.

We can also use the present tense to talk about future events that happen at a definite time or on a regular schedule. For example, you can say:

The movie begins at 7:30 tonight.
The office opens tomorrow morning at 9 A.M.
The train arrives at 6:15.
The store closes tonight at 10 P.M.

So, you don't need to be "tense" about the future! You can use both the present and the future tenses to talk about future time.

We hope this answers your question. Thanks for your letter, and good luck with your English!

Sincerely,

Side by Side

Global Exchange

NickyG: Hi. It's Sunday night here, and I just finished my biology homework. Before I turn off my computer, I want to tell you about my weekend. It was really great. I went camping with some of my friends. We left early Saturday morning and drove to the mountains. We hiked for several hours to a beautiful lake. We went swimming, we cooked over a campfire, and we slept outside. We told stories and sang songs until after midnight. In the morning, we made a big breakfast, we swam again, and then we packed up our things, hiked back to the car, and came home. How about you? How was your weekend? Write back soon. Okay?

Smile9: Hi. It's Monday morning here. I'm sitting in the computer lab at my school, and your message just arrived! I'm happy to hear from you again. My weekend wasn't as exciting as yours. I have final exams in all my courses this week, so I stayed home and studied all weekend. But I'm really looking forward to next weekend. Our family is going to travel to the place where my parents grew up. We're having a big family reunion on Saturday. All my relatives will be there. We don't see them very often, so it will be a very special time. I'll tell you about it when I return. Oh. Here comes my teacher! I've got to go! Talk to you soon.

Send a message to a keypal. Tell about what you did last weekend. Tell about your plans for next weekend.

LISTENING

You Have Five Messages!

_e_ **1** Sarah   **a.** will be visiting his parents.

____ **2** Bob   **b.** will be studying.

____ **3** Paula   **c.** will be attending a wedding.

____ **4** Joe   **d.** will go to the party.

____ **5** Carla   **e.** will be taking her uncle to the hospital.

FUN with IDIOMS

Do You Know These Expressions?

_e_   **1.**   It's raining cats and dogs!

____   **2.**   What's cooking?

____   **3.**   I'm tied up right now.

____   **4.**   I'll give you a ring tomorrow.

____   **5.**   The English test was a piece of cake!

____   **6.**   The English test was no picnic!

a.   I'll call you.

b.   It was difficult.

c.   It was easy.

d.   What's new?

e.   It's raining very hard.

f.   I'm busy.

What Are They Saying?

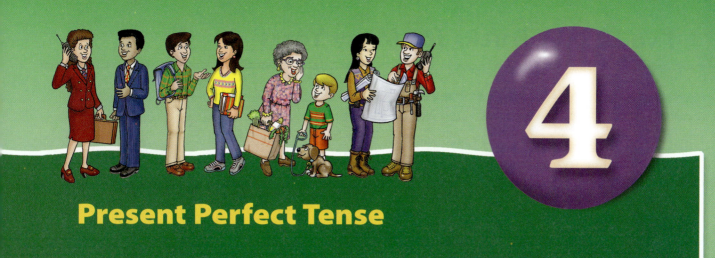

Present Perfect Tense

VOCABULARY PREVIEW

Things to Do Today

☐ 1. go to the bank

☐ 2. do the laundry

☐ 3. get a haircut

☐ 4. write to Grandma

☐ 5. take the dog for a walk

☐ 6. give the dog a bath

☐ 7. speak to the landlord

☐ 8. drive the kids to their dance lesson

☐ 9. eat lunch

☐ 10. ride my exercise bike

☐ 11. swim

☐ 12. see a movie

Things I've Done Today: I've . . .

☑ 1. gone to the bank
☑ 2. done the laundry
☑ 3. gotten a haircut
☑ 4. written to Grandma

☑ 5. taken the dog for a walk
☑ 6. given the dog a bath
☑ 7. spoken to the landlord
☑ 8. driven the kids to their dance lesson

☑ 9. eaten lunch
☑ 10. ridden my exercise bike
☑ 11. swum
☑ 12. seen a movie

I've Driven Trucks for Many Years

A. Do you know how to **drive** trucks?

B. Yes. I've **driven** trucks for many years.

1. *write reports*
written

2. *fly airplanes*
flown

3. *take X-rays*
taken

"Jambo!"

4. *speak Swahili*
spoken

5. *eat with chopsticks*
eaten

6. *give injections*
given

7. *draw cartoons*
drawn

8. *do yoga*
done

9. *ride horses*
ridden

I've Never Eaten Lunch with the Boss

A. I'm going to **eat** lunch with the boss tomorrow.

B. I'm jealous. I've never **eaten** lunch with the boss.

1. *fly in a helicopter*
flown

2. *see a Broadway show*
seen

3. *go on a cruise*
gone

4. *sing at the White House*
sung

5. *swim at the Ritz Hotel*
swum

6. *get a raise*
gotten

7. *be on television*
been

8. *take a ride in a hot-air balloon*
taken

9. *ride in a limousine*
ridden

Have You Ever Seen a Rainbow?

see
saw
seen

see a rainbow

A. Have you ever **seen** a rainbow?

B. Yes, I have. I **saw** a rainbow last year.

go
went
gone

1. *go scuba diving*

give
gave
given

2. *give a speech*

wear
wore
worn

3. *wear a kimono*

eat
ate
eaten

4. *eat cotton candy*

take
took
taken

5. *take a first-aid course*

fall
fell
fallen

6. *fall asleep in class*

be
was
been

7. *be in the hospital*

get
got
gotten

8. *get stuck in an elevator*

Have You Written the Report Yet?

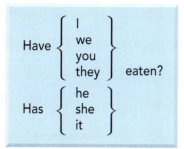

Have { I / we / you / they } eaten?

Has { he / she / it }

Yes, { I / we / you / they } have.

{ he / she / it } has.

write the report

write
wrote
written

A. Have you **written** the report yet?

B. Yes, I have. I **wrote** the report a little while ago.

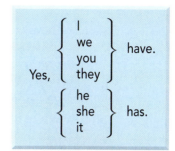

go to the bank

go
went
gone

A. Has David **gone** to the bank yet?

B. Yes, he has. He **went** to the bank a little while ago.

drive
drove
driven

1. *you*
drive the new van

give
gave
given

2. *Nancy*
give her presentation

get
got
gotten

3. *the employees*
get their paychecks

take
took
taken

4. *you and Robert*
take inventory

meet
met
met

5. *George*
meet the new boss

explain
explained
explained

6. *I*
explain the present perfect tense

He's Already Gone Bowling This Week

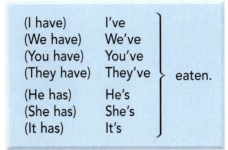

(I have)	I've	
(We have)	We've	
(You have)	You've	
(They have)	They've	} eaten.
(He has)	He's	
(She has)	She's	
(It has)	It's	

go
went
gone

A. Why isn't Charlie going to **go** bowling tonight?

B. He's already **gone** bowling this week.

A. Really? When?

B. He **went** bowling yesterday.

see
saw
seen

1. Why isn't Vicky going to see a movie this evening?

eat
ate
eaten

2. Why aren't Mr. and Mrs. Kendall going to eat at a restaurant tonight?

get
got
gotten

3. Why isn't Roy going to get a haircut today?

give
gave
given

4. Why aren't you going to give blood today?

take
took
taken

5. Why isn't Shirley going to take her children to the zoo this afternoon?

drive
drove
driven

7. Why aren't you and your family going to drive to the mountains today?

do
did
done

9. Why isn't Gary going to do his laundry today?

buy
bought
bought

11. Why aren't you going to buy bananas today?

wash
washed
washed

13. Why isn't Jim going to wash his car this morning?

wear
wore
worn

6. Why isn't Fred going to wear his purple tie today?

write
wrote
written

8. Why isn't Julie going to write to her best friend today?

swim
swam
swum

10. Why aren't your parents going to swim at the health club today?

have
had
had

12. Why aren't Mr. and Mrs. Davis going to have spaghetti for dinner tonight?

play
played
played

14. Why isn't your grandmother going to play Bingo today?

READING

WE CAN'T DECIDE

My friends and I can't decide what to do tonight. I don't want to see a movie. I've already seen a movie this week. Maggie doesn't want to go bowling. She has already gone bowling this week. Mark doesn't want to eat at a restaurant. He has already eaten at a restaurant this week. Betty and Mike don't want to play cards. They have already played cards this week. And NOBODY wants to go dancing. We have all gone dancing this week.

It's already 9 P.M., and we still haven't decided what we're going to do tonight.

ROLE PLAY

You and other students are the people in the story above. Create a role play based on the situation. Use these lines to start your conversation.

A. Look! It's already 9 P.M., and we still haven't decided what we're going to do tonight. Does anybody have any ideas?
B. I don't know.
C. Do you want to see a movie?
D. No, not me. I've already . . .
E. Does anybody want to . . . ?
F. I don't. I've already . . .
G. I have an idea. Let's . . .
H. No, I don't want to do that. I've already . . .

COMPLETE THE STORY

Fill in the correct words to complete the story.

Alvin has a very bad cold. He has been sick all week. He has tried very hard to get rid of his cold, but nothing he has done has helped. At the beginning of the week, he went to a clinic and saw a doctor. He followed the doctor's advice all week. He stayed home, took aspirin, drank* orange juice, ate chicken soup, and rested in bed.

At this point, Alvin is extremely frustrated. Even though he has _____¹ to a clinic and _____² a doctor, _____³ home, _____⁴ aspirin, _____⁵ orange juice, _____⁶ chicken soup, and _____⁷ in bed, he STILL has a very bad cold. Nothing he has _____⁸ has helped.

* drink – drank – drunk

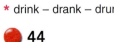

They Haven't Had the Time

I We You They	haven't (have not)
He She It	hasn't (has not)

eaten.*

A. Do you like to **swim**?

B. Yes, but I haven't **swum** in a long time.

A. Why not?

B. I haven't had the time.

A. Does Rita like to **draw**?

B. Yes, but she hasn't **drawn** in a long time.

A. Why not?

B. She hasn't had the time.

1. Do you like to ride your bicycle?

2. Does Arthur like to write poetry?

3. Does Kathy like to go kayaking?

4. Do you and your brother like to play Monopoly?

5. Does Laura like to make her own clothes?

6. Do you like to see your old friends?

7. Do Mr. and Mrs. Bell like to take dance lessons?

8. Does Grandpa like to do magic tricks?

9.

* In the present perfect tense, the word after **have** or **has** is a past participle. Some past participles are the same as the past tense (for example, **played**, **washed**, **made**). Other past participles are different from the past tense (for example, **swum**, **drawn**, **ridden**). We will tell you when the past participles are different. A list of these words is in the Appendix at the end of the book.

45

Has Timmy Gone to Bed Yet?

Have	I / we / you / they	eaten?
Has	he / she / it	

No,	I / we / you / they	haven't.
	he / she / it	hasn't.

A. Has Timmy gone to bed yet?

B. No, he hasn't. He has to go to bed now.

1. *Amanda*
do her homework

2. *you*
take your medicine

3. *James*
get up

4. *Debbie and Danny*
leave for school

5. *Jennifer*
call her supervisor

6. *you*
write your term paper

7. *you and your sister*
feed the dog

8. *you*
speak to your landlord

9. *Harry*
pay his electric bill

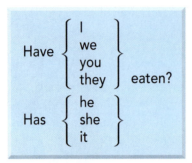
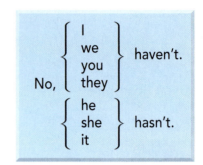

READING

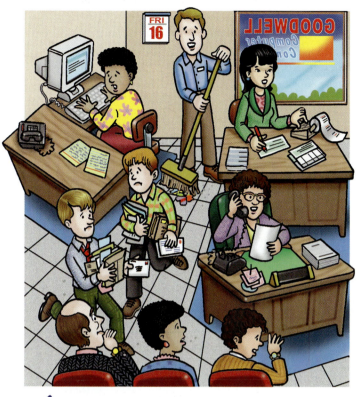

WORKING OVERTIME

I'm an employee of the Goodwell Computer Company. This is a typical Friday afternoon at our office. All the employees are working overtime. We haven't gone home because we haven't finished our work yet. Friday is always a very busy day.

The secretary still hasn't typed two important letters. The bookkeeper hasn't written all the paychecks. The office clerks haven't delivered all the mail. And the boss still hasn't spoken to three important people who are waiting to see her.

As for me, I'm the custodian, and I haven't finished my work yet either. I still haven't cleaned all the offices because my co-workers haven't gone home yet! I'm not really surprised. Friday is always a very busy day at our office.

✔ READING CHECK-UP

Q & A

The custodian at the Goodwell Computer Company is talking with the employees on a typical Friday afternoon. Using this model, create dialogs based on the story.

A. I see you haven't gone home yet.
B. No, I haven't. I still haven't *typed two important letters*.
A. Well, have a good weekend.
B. You, too.

WHAT'S THE WORD?

1. A. Have you (see) _____ the letter from the Lexon Company?
   B. Yes. I _____ it on your desk.

2. A. Have you (eat) _____ lunch yet?
   B. Yes. I _____ a few minutes ago.

3. A. Has the bookkeeper (go) _____ to the bank yet?
   B. Yes, she _____. She _____ there this morning.

4. A. Have you (speak) _____ to the boss about your vacation?
   B. Yes, I _____. I _____ to her about it yesterday.

5. A. Have you (make) _____ plans for my trip to Chicago yet?
   B. Yes. I _____ them yesterday.

6. A. Has anybody (read) _____ today's *New York Times*?
   B. Yes. I _____ it on my way to work.

7. A. Has the office clerk (take) _____ the mail to the post office yet?
   B. No, he _____. He _____ it to the mail room, but _____ _____ _____ it to the post office yet.

8. A. Has John (finish) _____ his work?
   B. Yes, he _____. He's already (go) _____ home.

Have You Seen Any Good Movies Recently?

A. Have you seen any good movies recently?

B. Yes, I have. I saw a very good movie last week.

A. Really? What movie did you see?

B. I saw *The Wedding Dancer*.

A. Oh. How was it?

B. It was excellent. It's one of the best movies I've ever seen.

A. Have you _____ any good _____s recently?

B. Yes, I have. I _____ a very good _____ last week.

A. Really? What _____ did you _____?

B. I _____ "_____."

A. Oh. How was it?

B. It was excellent. It's one of the best _____s I've ever _____.

1. *read • book*

2. *rent • video*

3. *go to • restaurant*

How to Say It!

Expressing Satisfaction

A. How was it?

B. {
It was excellent.
It was very good.
It was wonderful.
It was great.
It was fantastic.
It was terrific.
It was phenomenal.
It was awesome.
}

Practice the conversations in this lesson again. Express satisfaction in different ways.

READING

LINDA LIKES NEW YORK

Linda has lived in New York for a long time. She has done a lot of things in New York. She has gone to the top of the Empire State Building, she has visited the Statue of Liberty, she has taken a tour of the United Nations, and she has seen several Broadway shows.

However, there are a lot of things she hasn't done yet. She hasn't gone to any museums, she hasn't seen Ellis Island, and she hasn't been in Times Square on New Year's Eve.

Linda likes New York. She has done a lot of things, and there are still a lot more things to do.

LISTENING

Linda is on vacation in San Francisco. This is her list of things to do. Check the things on the list Linda has already done.

___ see the Golden Gate Bridge
___ visit Golden Gate Park
___ take a tour of Alcatraz prison
___ go to Chinatown
___ ride a cable car
___ eat at Fisherman's Wharf
___ buy souvenirs

Alan is a secretary in a very busy office. This is his list of things to do before 5 P.M. on Friday. Check the things on the list Alan has already done.

___ call Mrs. Porter
___ type the letter to the Mervis Company
___ take the mail to the post office
___ go to the bank
___ send an e-mail to the company's office in Denver
___ speak to the boss about my salary

It's Saturday, and Judy and Paul Johnson are doing lots of things around the house. This is the list of things they have to do today. Check the things on the list they've already done.

___ do the laundry
___ wash the kitchen windows
___ pay the bills
___ give the dog a bath
___ clean the garage
___ fix the bathroom sink
___ repair the fence
___ vacuum the living room rug

Make a List!

Make a list of things you usually do at school, at work, or at home. Then check the things you've already done this week. Share your list with other students. Tell about what you've done and what you haven't done.

PRONUNCIATION   Contractions with *is* & *has*

he is = he's	she is = she's
he has = he's	she has = she's

Listen. Then say it.

He is a good painter.

He has painted for a long time.

She is a good teacher.

She has taught for a long time.

Say it. Then listen.

He is a taxi driver.

He has driven a taxi for a long time.

She is an actress.

She has acted for a long time.

SIDE *by* **SIDE** **JOURNAL**

Think about your experiences in the place where you live. What have you done? What haven't you done yet? Write about it in your journal.

CHAPTER SUMMARY

GRAMMAR

PRESENT PERFECT TENSE

(I have)	I've	
(We have)	We've	
(You have)	You've	
(They have)	They've	eaten.
(He has)	He's	
(She has)	She's	
(It has)	It's	

I		
We	haven't	
You		
They		eaten.
He		
She	hasn't	
It		

Have	I we you they	eaten?
Has	he she it	

Yes,	I we you they	have.
	he she it	has.

No,	I we you they	haven't.
	he she it	hasn't.

KEY VOCABULARY

IRREGULAR VERBS

be – was/were – been	eat – ate – eaten	go – went – gone	swim – swam – swum
do – did – done	fall – fell – fallen	ride – rode – ridden	take – took – taken
draw – drew – drawn	fly – flew – flown	see – saw – seen	wear – wore – worn
drink – drank – drunk	get – got – gotten	sing – sang – sung	write – wrote – written
drive – drove – driven	give – gave – given	speak – spoke – spoken	

5

Present Perfect vs. Present Tense
Present Perfect vs. Past Tense
Since / For

- **Discussing Duration of Activity**
- **Medical Symptoms and Problems**
- **Career Advancement**
- **Telling About Family Members**

VOCABULARY PREVIEW

1. astronaut
2. cashier
3. clerk
4. computer programmer
5. doctor/physician
6. guidance counselor
7. guitarist
8. journalist
9. manager
10. musician
11. police officer
12. president
13. salesperson
14. taxi driver
15. vice president

How Long?

for	since
three hours	three o'clock
two days	yesterday afternoon
a week	last week
a long time	2000
•	•
•	•
•	•

A. How long have you known* each other?

B. We've known each other **for three years**.

*know – knew – known

A. How long have you been sick?

B. I've been sick **since last Friday**.

1. How long have Tom and Janet known each other?

   two years

2. How long have Mr. and Mrs. Garcia been married?

   1995

3. How long have you had a stomachache?
ten o'clock this morning

4. How long has Melanie had the measles?
five days

5. How long has Ms. Bennett been a guidance counselor?
nineteen years

6. How long have there been satellites in space?
1957

7. How long have you owned this car?
three and a half years

8. How long has Bob owned his own house?
1999

9. How long have you been interested in astronomy?
many years

10. How long has Glen been interested in photography?
a long time

11. How long have you been here?
1979

12. How long has your son had blue hair?
a week

53

A VERY DEDICATED DOCTOR

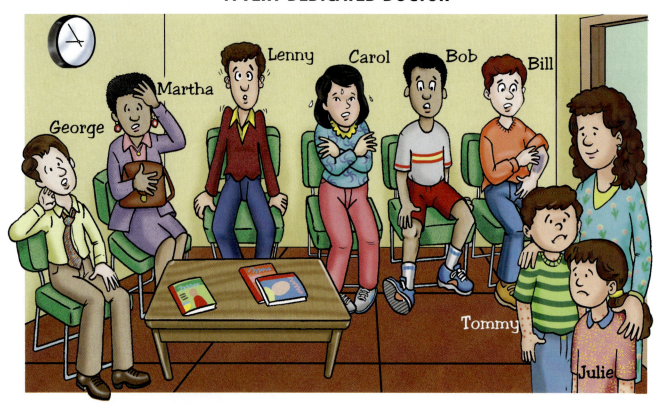

Dr. Fernando's waiting room is very full today. A lot of people are waiting to see him, and they're hoping that the doctor can help them. George's neck has been stiff for more than a week. Martha has had a bad headache since yesterday, and Lenny has felt dizzy since early this morning. Carol has had a high fever for two days, Bob's knee has been swollen for three weeks, Bill's arm has been black and blue since last weekend, and Tommy and Julie have had little red spots all over their bodies for the past twenty-four hours.

Dr. Fernando has been in the office since early this morning. He has already seen a lot of patients, and he will certainly see many more before the day is over. Dr. Fernando's patients don't know it, but he also isn't feeling well. He has had a pain in his back since last Thursday, but he hasn't taken any time to stay at home and rest. He has had a lot of patients this week, and he's a very dedicated doctor.

Q & A

Dr. Fernando's patients are talking to him about their problems. Using this model, create dialogs based on the story.

A. So how are you feeling today, *George*?
B. Not very well, Dr. Fernando.
A. What seems to be the problem?
B. *My neck is stiff.*
A. I see. Tell me, how long *has your neck been stiff?*
B. *For more than a week.*

CHOOSE

1. They've known each other since _____.
    a. 2000
    b. three years

2. I've been interested in astronomy for _____.
    a. last year
    b. one year

3. She has been a doctor for _____.
    a. two years ago
    b. two years

4. He has had a toothache since _____.
    a. yesterday
    b. two days

5. We've been here for _____.
    a. one hour
    b. one o'clock

6. There have been two robberies in our neighborhood since _____.
    a. one month
    b. last month

7. My grandparents have owned this house for _____.
    a. a long time
    b. many years ago

8. They've been in love since _____.
    a. last spring
    b. three months

CHOOSE

1. My right arm has been very _____.
    a. dizzy
    b. stiff

2. My son has a high _____.
    a. fever
    b. pain

3. Tell me, how long has your knee been _____?
    a. nauseous
    b. swollen

4. Ted's leg has been black and _____.
    a. blue
    b. red

5. Dr. Fernando, there are several patients in the _____.
    a. past 24 hours
    b. waiting room

6. Look! I have spots all over my _____!
    a. measles
    b. body

A. Do you know how to ski?

B. Yes. I've known how to ski **since I was a little girl**.

A. Are you two engaged?

B. Yes. We've been engaged **since we finished college**.

1. Does your sister Jennifer play the cello?

since she was eight years old

2. Is your friend Michael a professional musician?

since he graduated from music school

3. Do you have a personal computer?
since I started high school

4. Are you interested in modern art?
since I read about Picasso

5. Is Paul interested in Russian history?
since he visited Moscow

6. Does Timmy know how to count to ten?
since he was two years old

7. Do you like jazz?
since I was a teenager

8. Do you own your own business?
since I got out of the army

9. Do you know Mr. Wilson?
since I was a little boy

10. Do you have termites?
since we bought the house

11. Are you afraid of boats?
since I saw "Titanic"

12. Do your children know about "the birds and the bees"?*
since they were nine years old

*the facts of life

Have You Always Taught History?

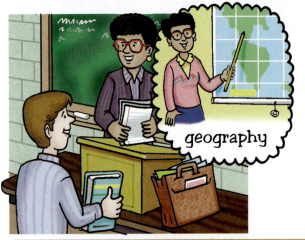

A. Have you always taught history?

B. No. **I've taught** history for the past three years. Before that, **I taught** geography.

A. Has Victor always been a taxi driver?

B. No. **He's been** a taxi driver since he immigrated to this country. Before that, **he was** an engineer.

1. Have you always liked classical music?
the past five years

2. Has Carlos always been the store manager?
last January

3. Has Kimberly always had short hair?
she started her new job

4. Has your son always wanted to be an astronaut?
the past five or six years

a New York accent

a cat

5. Has Ron always spoken with a southern accent?

he moved to Georgia

6. Have you and your wife always had a dog?

the last six months

whole milk

a bicycle

7. Have you always drunk skim milk?

I went on a diet

8. Has Carol always owned a sports car?

she won the lottery

How to Say It!

Reacting to Information

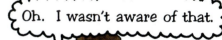

Oh. I didn't know that.

Oh. I didn't realize that.

Oh. I wasn't aware of that.

Practice the conversations in this lesson again. React to information in different ways.

How About You?

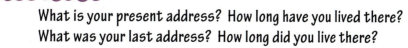

What is your present address? How long have you lived there?
What was your last address? How long did you live there?

Who is the leader of your country? How long has he/she been the leader?
Who was the last leader of your country? How long was he/she the leader?

Who is your English teacher now? How long has he/she been your teacher?
Who was your last English teacher? How long was he/she your teacher?

READING

A WONDERFUL FAMILY

Mr. and Mrs. Patterson are very proud of their family. Their daughter, Ruth, is a very successful engineer. She has been an engineer since she finished college. Her husband's name is Pablo. They have been happily married for thirty-five years. Pablo is a professional guitarist. He has known how to play the guitar since he was four years old.

Ruth and Pablo have two children. Their son, David, is a computer programmer. He has been interested in computers since he was a teenager. Their daughter, Rita, is a physician. She has been a physician since she finished medical school in 1997.

Mr. and Mrs. Patterson also have a son, Herbert. Herbert is single. He has been a bachelor all his life. He's a famous journalist. They haven't seen him since he moved to Singapore several years ago.

Mr. and Mrs. Patterson feel fortunate to have such wonderful children and grandchildren. They're very proud of them.

✔ READING CHECK-UP

TRUE OR FALSE?

1. Ruth got married thirty-five years ago.
2. Ruth's husband is a professional violinist.
3. Ruth and Pablo have two teenagers.
4. The Pattersons' grandson is interested in computers.

5. Rita has been in medical school since 1997.
6. Herbert has never been married.
7. Herbert hasn't seen his parents since they moved to Singapore several years ago.

LISTENING

Listen to the conversation and choose the answer that is true.

1. a. She doesn't have a backache now.
   b. She still has a backache.

2. a. His father is an engineer.
   b. His father isn't an engineer.

3. a. Her knee isn't swollen now.
   b. Her knee is still swollen.

4. a. He isn't a teenager.
   b. He's a teenager.

5. a. She has lived in Tokyo for five years.
   b. She lived in Tokyo for five years.

6. a. Roger lives in Cairo.
   b. Roger has lived in Cairo.

7. a. Amy went home two days ago.
   b. Amy hasn't been home for two days.

8. a. He has lived in Toronto for three years.
   b. He lived in Toronto for three years.

WORKING THEIR WAY UP TO THE TOP

Louis is very successful. For the past six years, he has been the manager of the Big Value Supermarket on Grant Street. Louis has worked very hard to get where he is today. First, he was a clerk for two years. Then, he was a cashier for three years. After that, he was an assistant manager for five years. Finally, six years ago, he became the manager of the store. Everybody at the Big Value Supermarket is very proud of Louis. He started at the bottom, and he has worked his way up to the top.

Kate is very successful. For the past two years, she has been the president of the Marcy Company. Kate has worked very hard to get where she is today. She started her career at the Marcy Department Store in Dallas, Texas. First, she was a salesperson for three years. Then, she was the manager of the Women's Clothing Department for ten years. Then, she was the store manager for eight years. After that, she moved to New York and became a vice president. Finally, two years ago, she became the president. Everybody at the Marcy Company is very proud of Kate. She started at the bottom, and she has worked her way up to the top.

 ## READING *CHECK-UP*

TRUE, FALSE, OR MAYBE?

Answer True, False, or Maybe (if the answer isn't in the story).

1. Louis started as a cashier at the Big Value Supermarket.
2. He has worked there for sixteen years.
3. All employees at the Big Value Supermarket start at the bottom.
4. Kate has been the manager of the Women's Clothing Department in Dallas for ten years.
5. The Women's Clothing Department was on the bottom floor of the store.
6. Kate hasn't been a vice president for two years.

Writing

Write a story about your English teacher.

How long have you known him/her?
How long has he/she been an English teacher?
What did he/she do before that? How long?

Where does he/she live?
How long has he/she lived there?
Has he/she lived anywhere else? Where?
   How long?

Besides teaching English, what is your English teacher interested in?
How long has he/she been interested in that?

A. George!

B. Tony! I can't believe it's you! I haven't seen you in years.

A. That's right, George. It's been a long time. How have you been?

B. Fine. And how about YOU?

A. Everything's fine with me, too.

B. Tell me, Tony, do you still live on Main Street?

A. No. I haven't lived on Main Street for several years. I live on River Road now.
And how about YOU? Do you still live on Central Avenue?

B. No. I haven't lived on Central Avenue since 1995. I live on Park Boulevard now.

A. Tell me, George, are you still a barber?

B. No. I haven't been a barber for several years. I'm a computer programmer now.
And how about YOU? Are you still a painter?

A. No. I haven't been a painter for a long time. I'm a carpenter now.

B. Tell me, Tony, do you still play the saxophone?

A. No. I haven't played the saxophone for many years. And how about YOU?
Do you still go fishing on Saturday mornings?

B. No. I haven't gone fishing on Saturday mornings since I got married.

A. Well, George, I'm afraid I have to go now. We should get together soon.

B. Good idea, Tony. It's been a long time.

Pretend that it's ten years from now. You're walking along the street and suddenly you meet a student who was in your English class. Try this conversation. Remember, you haven't seen this person for ten years.

A. _____!

B. _____! I can't believe it's you! I haven't seen you in years.

A. That's right, _____. It's been a long time. How have you been?

B. Fine. And how about YOU?

A. Everything's fine with me, too.

B. Tell me, _____, do you still live on _____?

A. No. I haven't lived on _____ (for/since) _____. I live on _____ now. And how about YOU? Do you still live on _____?

B. No. I haven't lived on _____ (for/since) _____. I live on _____ now.

A. Tell me, _____, are you still (a/an) _____?

B. No. I haven't been (a/an) _____ (for/since) _____. I'm (a/an) _____ now. And how about YOU? Are you still (a/an) _____?

A. No. I haven't been (a/an) _____ (for/since) _____. I'm (a/an) _____ now.

B. Tell me, _____, do you still _____?

A. No. I haven't _____ (for/since) _____. And how about YOU? Do you still _____?

B. No. I haven't _____ (for/since) _____.

A. Well, _____, I'm afraid I have to go now. We should get together soon.

B. Good idea, _____. It's been a long time.

PRONUNCIATION Reduced *have & has*

Listen. Then say it.

How long have you been sick?

How long has Ms. Bennett been a teacher?

Bob has been the manager for six months.

Say it. Then listen.

How long have you known each other?

How long has Mr. Perkins had a stomachache?

Kate has been the president for the past two years.

SIDE by SIDE JOURNAL

Write in your journal about your activities and interests. What sport or musical instrument do you play? How long have you known how to play it? Why do you like it? What other things are you interested in? How long have you been interested in those things? Why do you like them?

CHAPTER SUMMARY

GRAMMAR

SINCE/FOR

We've known each other	since	three o'clock. yesterday afternoon. last week. 2000. we were in high school.
	for	three hours. two days. a week. a long time.

PRESENT PERFECT VS. PRESENT TENSE

I **know** how to ski.

I've **known** how to ski since I was a little girl.

PRESENT PERFECT VS. PAST TENSE

Victor **was** an engineer.

He's **been** a taxi driver since he immigrated.

KEY VOCABULARY

OCCUPATIONS

astronaut
barber
carpenter
cashier
clerk
computer programmer
doctor/physician
engineer
guidance counselor

guitarist
journalist
manager
musician
painter

police officer
president
salesperson
taxi driver
vice president

MEDICAL CARE

black and blue
dizzy
doctor
fever
headache
measles

pain
patient
physician
stiff
stomachache
swollen

SUBJECTS

astronomy
geography
history
music
photography

🔴 **64**

Feature Article
Fact File
Around the World
Interview
We've Got Mail!

SIDE by SIDE Gazette

Global Exchange
Listening
Fun with Idioms
What Are They
Saying?

Volume 3   Number 2

"24/7"
24 Hours a Day/7 Days a Week

Work schedules are changing all over the world

A sign of the times

More and more companies around the world are operating twenty-four hours a day, seven days a week. Many of these companies do business with companies in other time zones around the world. Other companies sell products to customers worldwide. In an age of instant communication by telephone, by fax, and over the Internet, many businesses must stay open all the time to serve their customers. International banks, computer companies, manufacturing companies, and businesses that sell their products over the World Wide Web are examples of such companies.

Employees of these "24/7" companies have seen changes in their work schedules in recent years. About twenty percent of employees don't work on a traditional "9 to 5" daytime schedule anymore. Their companies have switched them to other shifts, such as 3:00 P.M. to 11:00 P.M., or 11:00 P.M. to 7:00 A.M. In the past, many factory workers, doctors and nurses, police, firefighters, and others had these shifts, but now many office workers have also started to work during these hours.

The night shift

Many local businesses have adjusted their hours to serve the employees of these companies. More and more supermarkets are open 24 hours a day. Restaurants and coffee shops close later and open earlier. And businesses such as photocopy centers, health clubs, laundromats, and even some child-care centers are always open.

Describe the work schedules of people you know. Are there any "24/7" businesses in your area? What's your opinion about these businesses and their employees' work schedules?

A typical night at the office

A health club that's open 24 hours a day

A coffee shop that never closes

Late-night shopper at the supermarket

Unique Jobs

Some jobs are unique. They exist only in certain countries.

a subway pusher in Japan

a tulip farmer in Holland

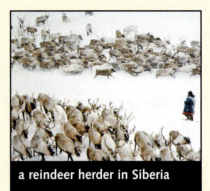
a reindeer herder in Siberia

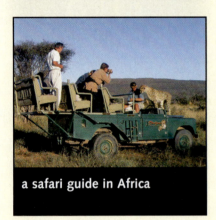
a safari guide in Africa

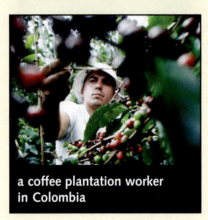
a coffee plantation worker in Colombia

a dog day-care worker in California

What unique jobs do you know? In what countries do these jobs exist?

Interview

Mr. and Mrs. Roberto Souza have two children, ages two and four. Mr. Souza works the day shift at a manufacturing company, and Mrs. Souza works at night in an office. Their lives are certainly busy!

Q: Mr. Souza, can you describe your typical day?

A: I get up at 5:30 A.M. I take a shower, eat breakfast, and make my lunch. Sometimes I do some laundry before I go to work. I leave the house at 6:30 A.M.

Q: Is anyone in your house awake when you leave?

A: No. Everyone is still asleep. I work from 7:00 A.M. until 3:00 P.M. After work, I pick up my kids at their grandmother's apartment. Usually we go food shopping and then we go home to make dinner. My wife has already left for work. I play with the kids, we eat dinner, and then I put the kids to bed. I'm normally asleep by 10:00 P.M.

Q: And Mrs. Souza, what about your day?

A: The kids and I get up at 7:00. We eat breakfast, and then they play while I do some housework. Sometimes we go to the park or we visit family or friends. Other times we go shopping. I take the kids to my mother's apartment at 2:00 P.M., and I'm at work by 3:00 P.M. I come home at 11:30 P.M. That's my day!

Q: It sounds exhausting! When do you have time to see your husband?

A: Sometimes he waits for me to come home, but usually he has already gone to bed. Believe it or not, we really see each other only on the weekends.

Q: Mr. Souza, what's the most difficult thing about your work schedule?

A: Communication. We leave each other notes and messages about bills, shopping, doctor's appointments, and everything else.

Q: And tell me, Mrs. Souza, is there anything good about these work schedules?

A: Yes. The children are always with a parent or a grandparent. They don't have to go to daycare, which is expensive. We know these schedules won't last forever. When the children are both in school, maybe we can each have a daytime job. I hope so!

FACT FILE

Vacation Time in Different Countries

Employees in different countries have different amounts of vacation time. What's the typical amount of vacation time employees receive in different countries you know? How do people usually spend their vacation time?

Weeks per Year

Australia	Germany	Denmark	Sweden	Japan	USA

Office Voice Mail

Hi Sam . . .

Has Sam . . .

		Yes	No
1	written a note to Mrs. Wilson?	___	___
2	called Mr. Chen?	___	___
3	sent an e-mail about the meeting?	___	___
4	spoken to the custodian?	___	___
5	made a list of the employees?	___	___
6	given the list to Ms. Baxter?	___	___
7	taken the package to the post office?	___	___

FUN with IDIOMS

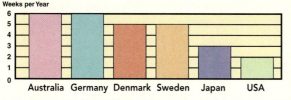
My new co-worker is a real peach.

She's the top banana in our company.

He's a real ham at office parties.

He's a couch potato.

She's a smart cookie.

He wants to ask for a raise, but he's chicken.

Do You Know These Expressions?

_d_ 1. My new co-worker is a real peach.

____ 2. She's the top banana in our company.

____ 3. He's a real ham at office parties.

____ 4. He's a couch potato.

____ 5. She's a smart cookie.

____ 6. He wants to ask for a raise, but he's chicken.

a. He's funny.

b. He's afraid.

c. She's intelligent.

d. He's nice.

e. He's lazy.

f. She's the boss.

We've Got Mail!

Dear Side by Side,

We are students in Mr. Smith's class at the English Language Center, and we are very confused! We just don't understand the present perfect tense. We don't have this tense in our languages. We don't know when to use it, and we really don't like all these past participles, such as "given" and "driven." Why do we need this tense anyway? Why can't we just use the tenses we already know?

Sincerely,
"Perfectly Happy with the Present and the Past"

Dear "Perfectly Happy,"

The present perfect tense has always been difficult for learners of English. We'll try to explain it to you with some examples.

We use the present perfect tense to talk about:

- things that happened (or didn't happen) sometime in the past, but the exact time isn't important. For example:

  I have (I've) already seen that movie.*
  He has (He's) never ridden a motorcycle.
  She hasn't gone to the bank yet.

* If the exact time IS important, we use the past tense: "I saw a movie yesterday."

- things that happened many times in the past. For example:

  I have (I've) driven trucks for many years.
  We have (We've) eaten lunch there many times.

- things that happened in the past and are still happening in the present. For example:

  I have (I've) known them for two years.
  She has (She's) been sick since last Thursday.
  They have (They've) lived here for a year.

It's interesting how different languages express time in different ways, and we can understand why this tense is difficult for you. In your languages, you might say:

✗ I live here since last year.
✗ I am living here since last year.
✗ I lived here since last year.

In English, these are all wrong. Sorry! The correct way to say this is:

✓ I have (I've) lived here since last year.

This means "I lived here before, and I still live here now."

So that's why we need the present perfect tense in English. Thanks for your question, and good luck!

Sincerely,
Side by Side

Global Exchange

Alex32: I'm sorry I haven't written for a while. I've been very busy. I've taken four exams this week, and I have to take one more tomorrow. This weekend I'm going to relax. I'm going to see the new Julia Richards movie. (My sister saw it last week, and she says it's one of the best movies she's ever seen.) I'm also going to eat dinner with my family at a new Indian restaurant. I'm looking forward to it. We haven't been to a restaurant in a long time, and I've never eaten Indian food. And I'm going to visit our city's modern art museum. Believe it or not, I've lived here all my life, and I've never gone there! So, how have you been? Have you seen any movies recently? Have you eaten at any restaurants? Have you gone to any interesting places?

Tell a keypal about some things you've done recently.

What Are They Saying?

6

Present Perfect Continuous Tense

- **Discussing Duration of Activity**
- **Reporting Household Repair Problems**
- **Describing Tasks Accomplished**
- **Reassuring Someone**
- **Describing Experiences**
- **Job Interviews**

VOCABULARY PREVIEW

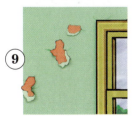

1. ask for a raise
2. complain
3. date
4. direct traffic
5. do sit-ups
6. leak
7. look for
8. mend
9. peel
10. pick apples
11. ring
12. stand in line

How Long Have You Been Waiting?

(I have)	I've	
(We have)	We've	
(You have)	You've	
(They have)	They've	been working.
(He has)	He's	
(She has)	She's	
(It has)	It's	

A. How long have you been waiting?

B. I've been waiting **for two hours**.

A. How long has your neighbor's dog been barking?

B. It's been barking **since this morning**.

1. How long has Yasmin been studying English?

eight months

2. How long have Mr. and Mrs. Green been living on School Street?

1994

3. How long has the phone been ringing?
two minutes

4. How long have you been feeling bad?
yesterday morning

5. How long have we been driving?
five hours

6. How long has it been snowing?
late last night

7. How long has Ted been having problems with his back?
high school

8. How long have you been practicing the piano?
half an hour

9. How long have Barry and Susan been dating?
three and a half years

10. How long has your baby son been crying?
early this morning

11. How long have I been running?
twenty minutes

12. How long have we been jogging?
about an hour

They've Been Arguing All Day

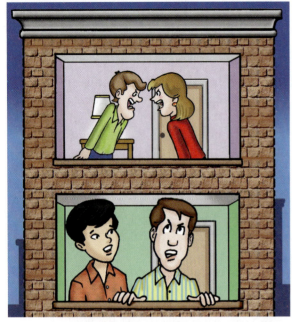

A. What are your neighbors doing?

B. They're arguing.

A. Have they been arguing for a long time?

B. Yes, they have. They've been arguing all day.*

*Or: all morning / all afternoon / all evening / all night

1. *you*
   studying

2. *Gary*
   exercising

3. *Brenda*
   waiting for the bus

4. *your parents*
   watching the news

5. *your car*
   making strange noises

6. *Officer Lopez*
   directing traffic

7. *Jim*
   looking for his keys

8. *you and your friends*
   standing in line for
   concert tickets

9.

APARTMENT PROBLEMS

Mr. and Mrs. Banks have been having a lot of problems in their apartment recently. For several weeks their bedroom ceiling has been leaking, their refrigerator hasn't been working, and the paint in their hallway has been peeling. In addition, they have been taking cold showers since last week because their water heater hasn't been working, and they haven't been sleeping at night because the heating system has been making strange noises.

Mr. and Mrs. Banks are furious. They have been calling the manager of their apartment building every day and complaining about their problems. He has been promising to help them, but they have been waiting for more than a week, and he still hasn't fixed anything at all.

✔ READING *CHECK-UP*

Q & A

Mr. and Mrs. Banks are calling the manager of their apartment building for the first time about each of the problems in their apartment. Using this model, create dialogs based on the story.

A. Hello.
B. Hello. This is *Mrs*. Banks.
A. Yes, *Mrs*. Banks. What can I do for you?
B. We're having a problem with *our bedroom ceiling*.
A. Oh? What's the problem?
B. *It's leaking*.
A. I see. Tell me, how long *has it been leaking?*
B. *It's been leaking for about an hour*.
A. All right, *Mrs*. Banks. I'll take care of it as soon as I can.
B. Thank you.

How About You?

Have you been having problems in your apartment or house recently? Tell about some problems you've been having.

A. You look tired. What have you been doing?

B. I've been writing letters since nine o'clock this morning.

A. Really? How many letters have you written?

B. Believe it or not, I've already written fifteen letters.

A. You're kidding! Fifteen letters?! NO WONDER you're tired!

A. Anthony looks tired. What has he been doing?

B. He's been making pizzas since ten o'clock this morning.

A. Really? How many pizzas has he made?

B. Believe it or not, he's already made seventy-five pizzas.

A. You're kidding! Seventy-five pizzas?! NO WONDER he's tired!

1. *you*
   plant flowers

2. *Ms. Perkins*
   give piano lessons

3. *Dr. Chen*
   see patients

4. *your grandmother*
   mend socks

5. *you*
   pick apples

6. *Tom and Sally*
   write thank-you notes

7. *Chester*
   take photographs

8. *Thelma*
   draw pictures

9. *you*
   go to job interviews

10. *Jackie*
    clean cages

11. *Rick*
    do sit-ups

12. *Dr. Harris*
    deliver babies

How to Say It!

Expressing Surprise

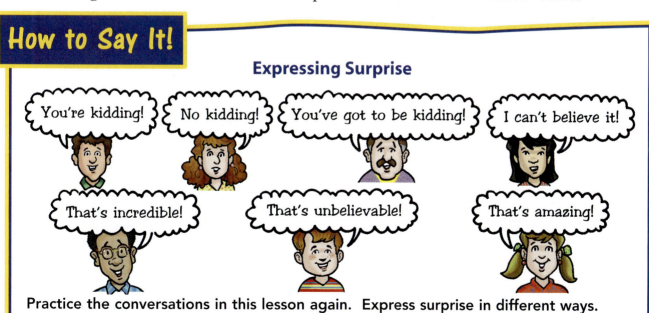

You're kidding!

No kidding!

You've got to be kidding!

I can't believe it!

That's incredible!

That's unbelievable!

That's amazing!

Practice the conversations in this lesson again. Express surprise in different ways.

There's Nothing to Be Nervous About!

A. I'm nervous.

B. Why?

A. I'm going to **fly in an airplane** tomorrow, and I've never **flown in an airplane** before.

B. Don't worry! I've been **flying in airplanes** for years. And believe me, there's nothing to be nervous about!

1. *drive downtown*

2. *give blood*

3. *buy a used car*

4. *do a chemistry experiment*

5. *run* in a marathon*

6. *go to a job interview*

*run – ran – run

 76

7. *speak at a meeting*

8. *sing in front of an audience*

9. *take a karate lesson*

10. *ask for a raise*

11. *go out on a date*

12.

INTERVIEW *Have You Ever . . . ?*

Interview other students in your class about experiences they have had. Ask these questions and make up your own questions. Then tell the class about these experiences.

Have you ever met a famous person?
(Who did you meet?)

Have you ever spoken at a meeting?
(Where did you speak? What did you say?)

Have you ever been in the hospital?
(Why were you there?)

Have you ever lost something important or
    valuable?
(What did you lose?)

Have you ever been very embarrassed?
(What happened?)

Have you ever been in an accident?
(What happened?)

Complete this conversation and act it out with another student.

A. Tell me, (Mr./Ms./Mrs./Miss _____), how long have you been living in _____?

B. I've been living in _____ (for/since) _____.

A. And where else have you lived?

B. I've also lived in _____.

A. Oh. How long did you live there?

B. I lived there for _____.

A. Okay. I see here on your resume that you're studying _____.

B. That's correct.

A. How long have you been studying _____?

B. (For/Since) _____.

A. Where?

B. At _____.

A. Tell me about your work experience. Where do you work now?

B. I work at _____.

A. How long have you been working there?

B. I've been working there (for/since) _____.

A. And what do you do there?

B. I _____.

A. And where did you work before that?

B. I worked at _____.

A. How long did you work there?

B. For _____.

A. What did you do?

B. I _____.

A. Well, I don't have any more questions.

B. I appreciate the opportunity to meet with you. Thank you very much.

A. It's been a pleasure. We'll call you soon.

READING

IT'S BEEN A LONG DAY

Frank has been assembling cameras since 7 A.M., and he's very tired. He has assembled 19 cameras today, and he has NEVER assembled that many cameras in one day before! He has to assemble only one more camera, and then he can go home. He's really glad. It's been a long day.

Julie has been typing letters since 9 A.M., and she's very tired. She has typed 25 letters today, and she has NEVER typed that many letters in one day before! She has to type only one more letter, and then she can go home. She's really glad. It's been a very long day.

Officer Jackson has been writing parking tickets since 8 A.M., and he's exhausted! He has written 211 parking tickets today, and he has NEVER written that many parking tickets in one day before! He has to write only one more parking ticket, and then he can go home. He's really glad. It's been an extremely long day.

 READING *CHECK-UP*

Q & A

Co-workers are talking with Frank, Julie, and Officer Jackson. Using this model, create dialogs based on the story.

A. *Frank*, you look tired.
B. I am. I've been *assembling cameras* since 7 A.M.
A. Really? How many *cameras* have you *assembled*?
B. Believe it or not, I've already *assembled 19 cameras* today.
A. That's a lot of *cameras*!
B. I know. I've never *assembled* that many *cameras* in one day before!

LISTENING

WHICH WORD DO YOU HEAR?

Listen and choose the correct answer.

1. a. gone   b. going
2. a. written   b. writing
3. a. seen   b. seeing
4. a. taken   b. taking
5. a. given   b. giving
6. a. driven   b. driving

WHO IS SPEAKING?

Listen and decide who is speaking.

1. a. a landlord   b. a boss
2. a. a student   b. a teacher
3. a. a singer   b. a dentist
4. a. a window washer   b. a baby-sitter
5. a. a doctor   b. a bookkeeper
6. a. a movie theater   b. a police officer
       cashier

Listen. Then say it.

I've been working for two hours.

She's been waiting for the bus.

Have you been studying for a long time?

Say it. Then listen.

He's been jogging for thirty minutes.

We've been looking for our keys.

Has she been exercising for a long time?

Write in your journal about places where you have lived, worked, and gone to school.

Where do you live now? How long have you been living there? Where else have you lived? How long did you live there?

Where do you work or go to school now? How long have you been working or going to school there? Where else have you worked or gone to school? How long did you work or study there? What did you do? What did you study?

CHAPTER SUMMARY

GRAMMAR

PRESENT PERFECT CONTINUOUS TENSE

(I have) (We have) (You have) (They have)	I've We've You've They've	been working.
(He has) (She has) (It has)	He's She's It's	

Have	I we you they	been working?
Has	he she it	

Yes,	I we you they	have.
	he she it	has.

KEY VOCABULARY

ACTIONS AND ACTIVITIES

argue	deliver *babies*	fly	live	practice	study
ask for *a raise*	direct traffic	give blood	look for	promise	take a *karate*
assemble	do a *chemistry*	give *piano* lessons	lose	ring	lesson
bark	experiment	go out on a date	make *pizzas*	run	take photographs
buy	do sit-ups	go to a job interview	make *strange*	see patients	type
call	draw pictures	have a problem with	*noises*	sing	wait
clean	drive	have problems with	mend *socks*	sleep	wait for
complain	exercise	help	peel	snow	watch *the news*
cry	feel bad	jog	pick *apples*	speak	work
date	fix	leak	plant *flowers*	stand in line	write *thank-you*
					notes

Gerunds
Infinitives
Review: Present Perfect and Present Perfect Continuous Tenses

VOCABULARY PREVIEW

1. enjoy / like
2. hate / can't stand
3. avoid
4. begin / start
5. continue / keep on
6. quit / stop
7. consider / think about
8. decide
9. learn
10. practice

My Favorite Way to Relax

to watch	watching
to dance	dancing
to swim	swimming

A. Do you **like to watch TV**?

B. Yes. I **enjoy watching TV** very much.
Watching TV is my favorite way to relax.

1. *you*
paint

2. *Beverly*
knit

3. *Kevin*
swim

4. *your parents*
play golf

5. *you and your friends*
dance

6. *you*
listen to music

7. *Hector*
go to the movies

8. *Valerie*
browse the web

9.

ENJOYING LIFE

Howard enjoys reading. He likes to read in the park. He likes to read in the library. He even likes to read in the bathtub! As you can see, reading is a very important part of Howard's life.

Patty enjoys singing. She likes to sing in school. She likes to sing in church. She even likes to sing in the shower! As you can see, singing is a very important part of Patty's life.

Brenda enjoys watching TV. She likes to watch TV in the living room. She likes to watch TV in bed. She even likes to watch TV in department stores! As you can see, watching TV is a very important part of Brenda's life.

Tom enjoys talking about politics. He likes to talk about politics with his friends. He likes to talk about politics with his parents. He even likes to talk about politics with his barber! As you can see, talking about politics is a very important part of Tom's life.

 ## READING *CHECK-UP*

Q & A

The people in the story are introducing themselves to you at a party. Using this model, create dialogs based on the story.

A. Hello. My name is *Howard*.
B. Nice to meet you. My name is _____.
    Are you enjoying the party?
A. Not really. To tell you the truth, I'd rather be *reading*.
B. Oh? Do you like to *read*?
A. Oh, yes. I enjoy *reading* very much.
B. I like to *read*, too. In fact, *reading* is my favorite way to relax.
A. Mine, too. Tell me, what do you like to *read*?
B. I like to *read books about famous people*. How about you?
A. I enjoy *reading short stories*.
B. Well, please excuse me. I have to go now. It was nice meeting you.
A. Nice meeting you, too.

She Hates to Drive Downtown

{ like **to** work }   { hate **to** work }   { ———— }
{ like work**ing** }   { hate work**ing** }   { avoid work**ing** }

A. Does Helen **like** { **to drive** / **driving** } downtown?

B. No. She **hates** { **to drive** / **driving** }* downtown.

She **avoids driving** downtown whenever she can.

* Or: can't stand { to drive / driving }

1. *Albert*
travel by plane

2. *you*
go to the mall

3. *your parents*
eat at fast-food restaurants

4. *Carmen*
sit in the sun

5. *you and your friends*
talk about politics

6. *Kathy*
use her cell phone

7. *you*
wear a suit and tie

8. *the president*
talk to reporters

9.

How About You?

What do you enjoy doing?
What do you avoid doing whenever you can?

BAD HABITS

Jill's co-workers always tell her to stop eating junk food. They think that eating junk food is unhealthy. Jill knows that, but she still keeps on eating junk food. She wants to stop, but she can't. Eating junk food is a habit she just can't break.

Vincent's friends always tell him to stop gossiping. They think that gossiping isn't nice. Vincent knows that, but he still keeps on gossiping. He wants to stop, but he can't. Gossiping is a habit he just can't break.

Jennifer's parents always tell her to stop interrupting people while they're talking. They think that interrupting people is very rude. Jennifer knows that, but she still keeps on interrupting people. She wants to stop, but she can't. Interrupting people is a habit she just can't break.

Walter's wife always tells him to stop talking about business all the time. She thinks that talking about business all the time is boring. Walter knows that, but he still keeps on talking about business. He wants to stop, but he can't. Talking about business is a habit he just can't break.

 ## READING *CHECK-UP*

Q & A

You're talking with the people in the story about their bad habits. Using this model, create dialogs based on the story.

A. *Jill?*
B. Yes?
A. You know . . . I don't mean to be critical, but I really think you should stop *eating junk food*.
B. Oh?
A. Yes. *Eating junk food is unhealthy*. Don't you think so?
B. You're right. The truth is . . . I want to stop, but I can't. *Eating junk food* is a habit I just can't break.

How About You?

Do you have any habits you "just can't break"? Tell about them.

How Did You Learn to Swim So Well?

| start **to** swim | learn **to** swim | ——— |
| start swimm**ing** | ——— | practice swimm**ing** |

A. How did you **learn to swim** so well?

B. Well, I **started** { **to swim** / **swimming** } when I was young,

and I've been **swimming** ever since.

A. I envy you. I've never **swum** before.

B. I'll be glad to teach you how.

A. Thank you. But isn't **swimming** very difficult?

B. Not at all. After you **practice swimming** a few times, you'll probably **swim** as well as I do.

A. How did you learn to _____ so well?

B. Well, I started $\begin{Bmatrix} \text{to _____} \\ \text{_____ing} \end{Bmatrix}$ when I was young,

and I've been _____ing ever since.

A. I envy you. I've never _____ before.

B. I'll be glad to teach you how.

A. Thank you. But isn't _____ing very difficult?

B. Not at all. After you practice _____ing a few times,

you'll probably _____ as well as I do.

1. *draw*

2. *box*

3. *surf*

4. *figure skate*

5. *tap dance*

6.

How to Say It!

Expressing Appreciation

Thank you.

I appreciate that.

That's very kind of you.

That's very nice of you.

Practice the conversations in this lesson again. Express appreciation in different ways.

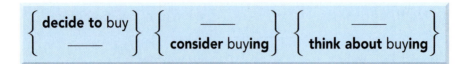

A. Guess what I've decided to do!

B. What?

A. I've **decided to get married**.

B. That's wonderful! How long have you been **thinking about getting married**?

A. For a long time, actually. I **considered getting married** a few years ago, but never did.

B. Well, I think you're making the right decision. **Getting married** is a great idea.

A. Guess what I've decided to do!

B. What?

A. I've decided to _____.

B. That's wonderful! How long have you been thinking about _____ing?

A. For a long time, actually. I considered _____ing a few years ago, but never did.

B. Well, I think you're making the right decision. _____ing is a great idea.

1. *get a dog*

2. *buy a new car*

3. *move to New York*

4. *go on a diet*

5. *go back to college*

6. *start my own business*

7. *retire*

8. *become a vegetarian*

9.

I've Made a Decision

{ **begin to** eat / **begin** eating }	{ —— / **keep on** eating }	{ —— / **quit** eating }
{ **start to** eat / **start** eating }	{ **continue to** eat / **continue** eating }	{ —— / **stop** eating }

begin = start keep on = continue quit = stop

A. I've made a decision.

B. What is it?

A. I've decided to **quit eating** junk food.

B. That's great! Have you ever tried to **stop eating** junk food before?

A. Yes. Many times. But every time I've **stopped eating** it,

I've **begun*** { **to eat** / **eating** } it again after a few days.

B. Well, I hope you're successful this time.

A. I hope so, too. After all, I can't **keep on eating** junk food for the rest of my life.

* begin – began – begun

A. I've made a decision.

B. What is it?

A. I've decided to quit* _____ing.

B. That's great! Have you ever tried to stop* _____ing before?

A. Yes. Many times. But every time I've stopped* _____ing,

I've begun* { to _____ / _____ing } again after a few days.

B. Well, I hope you're successful this time.

A. I hope so, too. After all, I can't keep on* _____ing for the rest of my life.

* quit = stop
  begin = start
  keep on = continue

1. *bite my nails*

2. *tease my little sister*

3. *worry about my health*

4. *argue with my neighbors*

5. *complain about my son-in-law*

6.

IMPORTANT DECISIONS

Jim had to make an important decision recently. He made an appointment for an interview at the Tektron Internet Company, and he had to decide what to wear. First, he considered wearing a sweater to the interview. Then, he thought about wearing a sports jacket. Finally, he decided to wear a suit and tie. Jim thinks he made the right decision. He's glad he didn't wear a sweater or sports jacket. He feels that wearing a suit and tie was the best thing to do.

Emily had to make an important decision recently. Her landlord sold her apartment building, and she had to decide where to move. First, she considered moving to another apartment. Then, she thought about buying a small house. Finally, she decided to move home with her parents for a while. Emily thinks she made the right decision. She's glad she didn't move to another apartment or buy a small house. She thinks that moving home with her parents for a while was the right thing to do.

Nick had to make an important decision recently. He got out of the army, and he had to decide what to do next with his life. First, he considered working in his family's grocery store. Then, he thought about taking a job in a restaurant. Finally, he decided to enroll in college and study engineering. Nick thinks he made the right decision. He's glad he didn't work in his family's grocery store or take a job in a restaurant. He feels that enrolling in college and studying engineering was the smartest thing to do.

Maria had to make an important decision recently. She lost her job as a bookkeeper because her company went out of business, and she had to decide what to do. First, she considered looking for another job as a bookkeeper. Then, she thought about working as a secretary for a while. Finally, she decided to enroll in technical school and study network programming. Maria thinks she made the right decision. She's glad she didn't look for another job as a bookkeeper or work as a secretary for a while. She thinks that enrolling in technical school and studying network programming was the best thing to do.

✔ READING CHECK-UP

TRUE, FALSE, OR MAYBE?

Answer True, False, or Maybe (if the answer isn't in the story).

1. Jim considered wearing a sweater to the interview.
2. He got the job at the Tektron Internet Company.
3. Emily decided not to move to another apartment.
4. Emily never considered buying a small house.
5. Emily's parents think that moving home was the right thing for her to do.
6. Nick's family is in the restaurant business.
7. Nick first became interested in engineering while he was in the army.
8. Maria wasn't a very good bookkeeper.
9. After Maria lost her job, she worked as a secretary for a while.
10. Maria feels she made the right decision.

LISTENING

Listen and choose the correct answer.

1. a. She enjoys going to the mall.
   b. She hates going to the mall.

2. a. He sold his car.
   b. He's going to sell his car.

3. a. He bites his nails.
   b. He stopped biting his nails.

4. a. She likes traveling by plane.
   b. She can't stand traveling by plane.

5. a. They're going to move to Florida.
   b. They might move to Florida.

6. a. He's married.
   b. He isn't married.

7. a. She's going to keep on practicing.
   b. She isn't going to continue practicing.

8. a. He interrupts people.
   b. He doesn't interrupt people any more.

Listen. Then say it.

I like to watch TV.

She hates to drive downtown.

How did you learn to draw?

I started to skate last year.

Say it. Then listen.

We decided to move.

He can't stand to wear a tie.

They've already begun to eat.

I continue to worry about my health.

SIDE by SIDE JOURNAL

Write in your journal about an important decision you had to make.

I had to make an important decision recently. _____,

and I had to decide what to do. First, I considered _____. Then, I thought about _____.

Finally, I decided to _____ because _____.

CHAPTER SUMMARY

GRAMMAR

VERB + INFINITIVE

| decide learn | to _____ |

VERB + GERUND

| avoid consider enjoy keep on practice quit stop think about | _____ing |

VERB + INFINITIVE / GERUND

| begin can't stand continue hate like start | to _____ _____ing |

GERUND AS SUBJECT

Watching TV is my favorite way to relax.

GERUND AS OBJECT

I'm thinking about **getting married**.

KEY VOCABULARY

VERBS

begin / start	continue / keep on	avoid	box	interrupt	tap dance
can't stand / hate	enjoy / like	decide	figure skate	retire	tease
consider / think about	quit / stop	learn	gossip	surf	
		practice			

Past Perfect Tense
Past Perfect Continuous Tense

VOCABULARY PREVIEW

1. discuss
2. fly a kite
3. go canoeing
4. go window-shopping
5. pack

6. purchase
7. realize
8. shine
9. water
10. wrestle

11. forget
12. remember
13. memorize
14. rehearse
15. perform

They Didn't Want to

I
He
She
It
We
You
They
} had eaten.

the weekend before

A. Why didn't Mr. and Mrs. Henderson **see** a movie last weekend?

B. They didn't want to. They **had seen** a movie the weekend before.

the evening before

1. Why didn't your parents eat out yesterday evening?

the Saturday before

2. Why didn't Barry go canoeing last Saturday?

the morning before

3. Why didn't Martha make eggs for breakfast yesterday morning?

the night before

4. Why didn't you have pizza for dinner last night?

the Sunday before

5. Why didn't you and your friends drive to the beach last Sunday?

the day before

6. Why didn't Paul wear his polka dot shirt to work yesterday?

the semester before

7. Why didn't Susan take a psychology course last semester?

the month before

8. Why didn't your neighbors give a party last month?

the week before

9. Why didn't Mozart write an opera last week?

the Saturday afternoon before

10. Why didn't you go window-shopping last Saturday afternoon?

the day before

11. Why didn't Monica fly her kite yesterday?

the evening before

12. Why didn't you and your family discuss politics at the dinner table yesterday evening?

the weekend before

13. Why didn't George do card tricks for his friends last weekend?

14.

THE MOST IMPORTANT THING

Roger thought he was all prepared for his dinner party last night. He had sent invitations to his boss and all the people at the office. He had looked through several cookbooks and had found some very interesting recipes. He had even gone all the way downtown to buy imported fruit, vegetables, and cheese, which he needed for his dinner. However, as soon as Roger's doorbell rang and his guests arrived, he realized that he had forgotten to turn on the oven. Roger felt very foolish. He couldn't believe what he had done. He thought he was all prepared for his dinner party, but he had forgotten to do the most important thing.

Mr. and Mrs. Jenkins thought they were all prepared for their vacation. They had packed their suitcases several days ahead of time. They had gone to the bank and purchased traveler's checks. They had even asked their next-door neighbor to water their plants, feed their dog, and shovel their driveway if it snowed. However, as soon as Mr. and Mrs. Jenkins arrived at the airport, they realized that they had forgotten to bring their plane tickets with them, and there wasn't enough time to go back home and get them. Mr. and Mrs. Jenkins were heartbroken. They couldn't believe what they had done. They thought they were all prepared for their vacation, but they had forgotten to do the most important thing.

Harold thought he was all prepared for his job interview yesterday. He had gone to his barber and gotten a very short haircut. He had bought a new shirt, put on his best tie, and shined his shoes. He had even borrowed his brother's new suit. However, as soon as Harold began the job interview, he realized that he had forgotten to bring along his resume. Harold was furious with himself. He thought he was all prepared for his job interview, but he had forgotten to do the most important thing.

Janet thought she was all prepared for the school play. She had memorized the script several weeks in advance. She had practiced her songs and dances until she knew them perfectly. She had even stayed up all night the night before and rehearsed the play by herself from beginning to end. However, as soon as the curtain went up and the play began, Janet realized that she had forgotten to put on her costume. Janet was really embarrassed. She couldn't believe what she had done. She thought she was all prepared for the play, but she had forgotten to do the most important thing.

 READING *CHECK-UP*

TRUE, FALSE, OR MAYBE?

Answer True, False, or Maybe (if the answer isn't in the story).

1. Roger had remembered to buy the ingredients he needed.
2. Roger hadn't remembered to cook the food.
3. Roger's guests couldn't believe what he had done.
4. Mr. and Mrs. Jenkins had forgotten to buy their plane tickets.
5. When Mr. and Mrs. Jenkins realized what had happened, they felt very sad and upset.
6. Harold thinks it's important to bring a resume to a job interview.
7. Harold doesn't have a suit.
8. Janet hadn't seen the script until the night before the play.
9. Before the play began, Janet hadn't realized that she had forgotten to put on her costume.

WHICH IS CORRECT?

1. Before Barbara went on her vacation, she went to the bank and bought (tickets   traveler's checks).
2. Peter wanted his boss to come over for dinner, but he forgot to send him (a resume   an invitation).
3. Sheila (borrowed   bought) her roommate's laptop for a few days.
4. Our grandchildren were (heartbroken   foolish) when our dog ran away.
5. At the supermarket next to the United Nations, (imported   important) people buy (imported   important) food.

How About You?

Have you ever thought you were all prepared for something, but you realized you had forgotten to do something important?
What were you preparing for?
What had you done?
What had you forgotten to do?

They Didn't Get There on Time

A. Did you get to the **concert** on time?

B. No, I didn't. By the time I got to the **concert**, it had already **begun**.

1. *post office*
   closed

2. *plane*
   take off

3. *movie*
   start

4. *train*
   leave

5. *lecture*
   end

6. *meeting*
   finish

7. *library*
   close

8. *boat*
   sail away

9. *parade*
   go by

He Hadn't Gone Fishing in a Long Time

I
He
She
It
We
You
They
} hadn't eaten.
(had not)

A. Did Grandpa enjoy **going fishing** last weekend?

B. Yes, he did. He hadn't **gone fishing** in a long time.

1. Did Natalie enjoy swimming in the ocean last weekend?

2. Did you enjoy seeing a movie yesterday evening?

3. Did Mr. and Mrs. Ramirez enjoy taking a walk along the beach yesterday?

4. Did you and your friends enjoy eating at Burger Queen yesterday?

5. Did Henry enjoy singing with the choir last Sunday?

6. Did you enjoy having strawberry shortcake for dessert last night?

7. Did Jim and Tess enjoy riding on a roller coaster this afternoon?

8. Did Kevin enjoy playing "hide and seek" with his children last night?

9. Did Mrs. Kramer enjoy reading her old love letters last weekend?

DAYS GONE BY

Michael took a very special trip last month. He went back to Fullerton, his home town. Michael's visit to Fullerton was very special to him. He was born there, he grew up there, but he hadn't been back there since he finished high school.

He went to places he hadn't gone to in years. He walked through the park in the center of town and remembered the days he had walked through the same park with his first girlfriend. He passed by the empty field where he and his friends had played baseball every day after school. And he stood for a while in front of the movie theater and thought about all the Saturday afternoons he had spent there sitting in the balcony, watching his favorite movie heroes and eating popcorn.

He did things he hadn't done in a long time. He had some homemade ice cream at the ice cream shop, he rode on the merry-go-round in the park, and he went fishing at the lake on the outskirts of town. For a while, he felt like a kid again. He hadn't had homemade ice cream, ridden on a merry-go-round, or gone fishing since he was a young boy.

He also saw people he hadn't seen in years. He visited several of his old neighbors who had never moved out of the neighborhood. He said hello to the owners of the candy store near his house. And he even bumped into Mrs. Riley, his tenth-grade science teacher.

During his visit to his home town, Michael remembered places he hadn't gone to, things he hadn't done, and people he hadn't seen since his childhood. Michael's trip back to Fullerton was a very nostalgic experience for him. Going back to Fullerton brought back many memories of days gone by.

✔ READING CHECK-UP

TRUE, FALSE, OR MAYBE?

Answer True, False, or Maybe (if the answer isn't in the story).

1. Michael moved back to Fullerton last month.
2. He hadn't seen Fullerton in years.
3. When Michael passed by the field last month, children were playing baseball.
4. Michael enjoyed going to the movies when he was young.
5. The ice cream shop was near Michael's home in Fullerton.
6. Michael rode on the merry-go-round when he was a young boy.
7. Some of Michael's old neighbors still live in the same neighborhood.
8. Mrs. Riley still teaches science.

WHICH IS CORRECT?

1. I always enjoy eating Aunt Betty's (home town   homemade) food.
2. The new shopping mall is located in the (outskirts   outside) of our city.
3. She recently visited the town where she had (spent   grown up) her childhood.
4. I bumped (through   into) an old friend on the street the other day.
5. They hadn't been (back   by) to their old neighborhood in several years.
6. Seeing my old college friends was a (nauseous   nostalgic) experience for me.

LISTENING

Listen and choose the correct answer.

1. a. Yes. They've never eaten there.
   b. Yes. They had never eaten there.

2. a. I had already seen it.
   b. I've already seen it.

3. a. No. It had already started.
   b. No. It has already started.

4. a. But I had already done it.
   b. But I've already done it.

5. a. She had memorized all the important names and dates.
   b. She's going to study very hard.

6. a. Have you ever stayed there before?
   b. Had you ever stayed there before?

THINK ABOUT IT! *Feelings and Experiences*

Think about times you have had these feelings. Share your experiences with other students.

I was heartbroken when . . .

I was furious when . . .

I felt foolish when . . .

I always feel nostalgic when . . .

103

Have You Heard About Harry?

A. Have you heard about Harry?

B. No, I haven't. What happened?

A. He broke his leg last week.

B. That's terrible! How did he do THAT?

A. He was roller-skating . . . and he had never roller-skated before.

B. Poor Harry! I hope he feels better soon.

A. Have you heard about _____?

B. No, I haven't. What happened?

A. (He/She) _____ last week.

B. That's terrible! How did (he/she) do THAT?

A. (He/She) was _____ing . . . and (he/she) had never _____ before.

B. Poor _____! I hope (he/she) feels better soon.

1. *twist his ankle*
fly a kite

2. *injure her knee*
ski

3. *burn himself*
bake brownies

4. *sprain her wrist*
play squash

5. *get a black eye*
box

6. *hurt her arm*
wrestle

7. *lose his voice*
sing opera

8. *dislocate her shoulder*
do gymnastics

9. *get hurt in an accident*
ride a motorcycle

10. *sprain his back*
do the tango

11. *break his front teeth*
chew on a steak bone

12.

How to Say It!

Sharing News About Someone

A. { Have you heard about
Have you heard the news about } *Harry?*
Have you heard what happened to

B. No, I haven't. What happened?

Practice the conversations in this lesson again. Begin your conversations in different ways.

It's Really a Shame

I He She It We You They	had been eating.

A. I heard that Arnold failed his driver's test last week. Is it true?

B. Yes, it is . . . and it's really a shame. He had been practicing for a long time.

A. I heard that _____ last week. Is it true?

B. Yes, it is . . . and it's really a shame. (He / She / They) had been _____ing for a long time.

I heard that . . .

1. Fred lost his job at the factory
work there

2. Larry and Jane broke up
go together

3. Mona had to cancel her trip to France
plan it

4. Pam and Bob canceled their wedding
plan to get married

5. Mr. and Mrs. Williams moved
live in this neighborhood

6. Walter had another heart attack
feel better

7. Alex did poorly on his science exam
study for it

8. Penny twisted her ankle and couldn't run in the marathon
train for it

9. Your daughter got sick and couldn't perform in her piano recital
rehearse for it

10. Herbert caught a cold and couldn't go camping
look forward to it

THEIR PLANS "FELL THROUGH"

Patty had planned to have a party last weekend. She had been getting ready for the party for a long time. She had invited all of her friends and several co-workers, she had cooked lots of food, and she had cleaned her apartment from top to bottom. But at the last minute, she got sick and had to cancel the party. Poor Patty! She was really disappointed.

John and Julia had planned to get married last month. They had been planning their wedding for more than a year, and all of their friends and relatives had been looking forward to the ceremony. Julia had bought a beautiful wedding gown, John had rented a fancy tuxedo, and they had sent invitations to 150 people. But at the last minute, John "got cold feet"* and they had to cancel the wedding.

* got scared

Michael had planned to ask his boss for a raise last week. He had been preparing to ask his boss for a raise for a long time. He had come to work early for several weeks, he had worked late at the office every night, and he had even bought a new suit to wear to the appointment with his boss. Unfortunately, before Michael could even ask for a raise, his boss fired him.

IN YOUR OWN WORDS

FOR WRITING AND DISCUSSION

Tell about plans YOU had that "fell through."

What had you planned to do?
How long had you been planning to do it?
What had you done beforehand?
What went wrong? What happened?
Were you upset? disappointed?

When Stella Karp won the marathon last week, nobody was surprised. She had been getting up early and jogging every morning. She had been eating health foods and taking vitamins for several months. And she had been swimming fifty laps every day after work. Stella Karp really deserved to win the marathon. After all, she had been preparing for it for a long time.

When my friend Stuart finally passed his driver's test the other day, nobody was surprised. He had been taking lessons at the driving school for several months. He had been practicing driving with his father for the past several weeks. And he had been studying the "rules of the road" since he was a little boy. My friend Stuart really deserved to pass his driver's test. After all, he had been preparing for it for a long time.

When Sally Compton got a promotion last week, nobody was surprised. She had been working overtime every day for several months. She had been studying computer programming in the evening. And she had even been taking extra work home on the weekends. Sally Compton really deserved to get a promotion. After all, she had been working hard to earn it for a long time.

We all feel proud when we accomplish something that we have prepared for. Tell other students about an accomplishment you're proud of.

Write in your journal about something you accomplished: What did you accomplish? How long had you been preparing for it? How had you been preparing?

Listen. Then say it.

She had seen a movie the day before.

We had never roller-skated before.

It had already begun.

Patty had planned to have a party.

Say it. Then listen.

He had gone fishing the week before.

We had been studying for several hours.

I had forgotten to do it.

Tom had been practicing for a long time.

CHAPTER SUMMARY

GRAMMAR

PAST PERFECT TENSE

I He She It We You They	had eaten.

I He She It We You They	hadn't eaten.

PAST PERFECT CONTINUOUS TENSE

I He She It We You They	had been eating.

KEY VOCABULARY

ACTIONS AND ACTIVITIES

arrive	do	get married	jog	rehearse	take a *psychology*
ask	do *card* tricks	get ready	know	remember	course
ask for a raise	do gymnastics	get sick	leave	rent	take a trip
bake	do poorly	get up	live	ride	take a walk
begin	do the *tango*	give a party	look forward to	ring	take home
believe	drive	go	look through	roller-skate	take lessons
borrow	earn	go back	lose	run	take off
box	eat	go by	make *eggs*	sail away	take vitamins
break	eat out	go camping	memorize	say hello	think
break up	end	go canoeing	move	see	think about
bring	enjoy	go downtown	move out	see a movie	train
bring along	fail	go fishing	need	send	turn on
bring back	fall through	go together	pack	shine	twist
bump into	feed	go up	pass	shovel	visit
buy	feel	go window-	pass by	sing	walk
cancel	feel better	shopping	perform	sit	watch
catch a cold	find	grow up	plan	ski	water
chew	finish	happen	play	snow	wear
clean	fire	have *pizza*	play *squash*	spend	win
close	fly *her* kite	hear	practice	sprain	work
come to work	forget	hope	prepare	stand	work late
cook	get	hurt *her arm*	purchase	start	work overtime
deserve	get a promotion	hurt *himself*	put on	stay up	wrestle
discuss	get cold feet	injure	read	study	write
dislocate	get hurt	invite	realize	swim	

Feature Article Fact File Around the World Interview We've Got Mail!	SIDE by SIDE Gazette	Global Exchange Listening Fun with Idioms What Are They Saying?

Volume 3   Number 3

The Jamaican Bobsled Team

Amazing athletes from a Caribbean island

An unusual group of athletes arrived in Calgary, Canada for the 1988 Winter Olympic Games—the Jamaican Bobsled Team. Many people were surprised. How could the Caribbean island of Jamaica have a bobsled team? Jamaica doesn't have any snow!

The Jamaican athletes had never competed in the Winter Olympics before. In fact, most of them hadn't ever been on a bobsled or seen snow before they began to prepare for the Olympics. But by the time the team members arrived in Calgary, they had trained hard for their first Olympic event. They had been running and weight training in Jamaica. Then they had gone to a training center in Lake Placid, New York. Unfortunately, they had poor equipment, and their bobsled crashed a lot during training.

They didn't do well in the Olympics. Most people were sure they had seen the Jamaican Bobsled Team for the first and last time! But the team didn't give up. They had lost, but they had been in the Olympics, and they wanted to go back and compete again.

The team went to a special training center in Germany. They trained there four to eight hours a day. By the time these athletes arrived at the 1994 Olympic Winter Games in Norway, they had become a much stronger bobsled team. They had practiced for years. They were also very famous because a movie about the team, *Cool Runnings*, had been in theaters around the world the year before.

At the 1994 games, the team came in 14th in the four-person bobsled event, and they placed 10th in the two-person event. The team had done the impossible! They had competed well in the Olympics, and they had won the hearts of fans around the world.

The movie *Cool Runnings* tells the story of a Jamaican bobsled team at the Olympics. The movie is part fact and part fiction. The popular movie soundtrack has reggae music by famous Jamaican musicians.

The first modern Olympics were in Athens, Greece in 1896. Now there are Summer Olympics and Winter Olympics every four years. Athletes represent their countries in different events. Summer Olympic events include track, gymnastics, and swimming. Winter Olympic events include skiing, skating, and the bobsled competition.

Children and Sports Training

In different countries around the world, children begin training at an early age to compete in different popular sports.

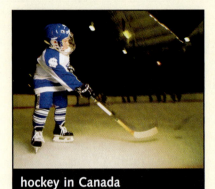

hockey in Canada

baseball in Japan

soccer in Brazil

gymnastics in Russia

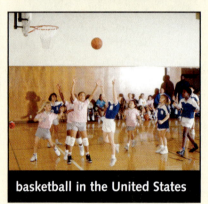

basketball in the United States

distance running in Kenya

What sports are popular in your country? At what age do children start training to compete in these sports?

Interview

A Side by Side Gazette reporter interviewed Olga Petrova last week. Olga had just won the Women's Regional Figure Skating Competition.

Q: Olga, I'm sure you're very happy about today's competition.

A: Oh, yes. I'm very happy. You know, I had been preparing for this day for a long time.

Q: How had you been preparing?

A: In the months before the competition, I had been training with my coach ten hours a day. I had been getting up early, and I had been practicing my routines over and over again.

Q: When did you first know you wanted to compete as a skater?

A: I began to skate back in Russia when I was four years old. By the time I was seven, I had already skated in many competitions, and I had won several medals. We moved here when I was ten, and I began to take lessons at a skating program in our city. By the time I was eleven, I had finished all the levels of this program. My parents found a professional coach, Mr. Gary Abrams, and I've been training with him ever since.

Q: Now that you have won this regional competition, what's next?

A: The National Competition. It's in three months. I have to work very hard to prepare for that. My dream is to be in the Olympics next winter. I must do very well in the Nationals.

Q: Good luck, Olga! We'll see you in the Olympics!

A: Oh, I hope so.

FACT FILE

Countries in the Olympics

Only 14 countries competed in the first modern Olympics in 1896. Over the years, the number of participating countries has grown. Does your country compete in the summer or winter games? In which events does your country do well?

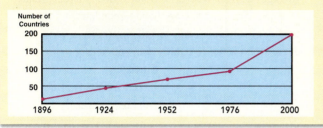

Olympic Game Highlights

_b_ **1**	**a.**	figure skating
___ **2**	**b.**	basketball
___ **3**	**c.**	running
___ **4**	**d.**	gymnastics
___ **5**	**e.**	swimming

FUN with IDIOMS

Do You Know These Expressions?

_c_ **1.** Break a leg!		**a.**	Don't be sad!
___ **2.** Hold your tongue!		**b.**	Try hard!
___ **3.** Keep your chin up!		**c.**	Good luck!
___ **4.** Keep your eye on the ball!		**d.**	Pay attention!
___ **5.** Put your best foot forward!		**e.**	Don't bother me!
___ **6.** Get off my back!		**f.**	Be quiet!

Dear Side by Side,

I have a question about gerunds and infinitives after verbs. I'm very confused. I know that after some verbs, I must use a gerund, such as "practice swimming" and "consider buying." After other verbs, I must use an infinitive, such as "learn to swim" and "decide to buy." And finally, I know that after some verbs, I can use either a gerund or an infinitive, such as "like to swim" and "like swimming." Are there any rules that will tell me what to do with different verbs?

Sincerely,
"Worrying About the Rules"

Dear Side by Side,

We've been studying the present perfect and present perfect continuous tenses in our class for the past several weeks. I think I finally understand this grammar, but now we have begun learning the past perfect tense, and to tell the truth, I don't understand when to use it. Can you help?

Sincerely,
"Life Was Perfect Before the Past Perfect"

Dear "Worrying About the Rules,"

You seem to understand how to use gerunds and infinitives. Unfortunately, we're sorry to tell you that there aren't any rules about what to do with different verbs. You just have to learn about each verb. Keep on practicing gerunds and infinitives, and stop worrying about the rules! Using these verbs is a lot better than thinking about them too much! Good luck!

Sincerely,

Dear "Life Was Perfect,"

We understand your problem because we use both the present perfect and past perfect tenses to talk about things that happened in the past. Here's the difference. We use the present perfect tense to talk about things that happened before now. For example:

I don't want to see that movie today.
I have already seen it.

We use the past perfect tense to talk about things that happened before another time in the past. For example:

I didn't want to see that movie yesterday.
I had already seen it.

We're glad you have learned the present perfect tense, and we're sure you'll do well with the past perfect!

Best wishes,

Global Exchange

Stamp4: Have I told you about my hobby? I've been collecting stamps since I was a little kid. I began to collect stamps when I was eight years old. At that time, my mother worked at an international bank. Every Friday, she brought home stamps from all the letters she had received during that week. I also had many penpals in different countries, and we wrote letters to each other very often. By the time I was twelve, I had collected more than 1000 stamps from 50 different countries! I've continued collecting stamps, but now it's more difficult. My mother retired from her job, and my penpals send me e-mail messages instead of letters. (The Internet has been very bad for my stamp collection!) Tell me, do you have a hobby? What do you enjoy doing in your free time? How long have you been doing that? Write and tell me about it.

Send a message to a keypal. Tell about your favorite hobby.

What Are They Saying?

Two-Word Verbs:
Separable
Inseparable

VOCABULARY PREVIEW

1. cross out	6. pick out	11. throw away
2. fill out	7. put away	12. try on
3. hand in	8. put on	13. turn on
4. hang up	9. take down	14. turn off
5. hook up	10. take off	15. wake up

bring back the TV	**bring** it **back**
call up Sally	**call** her **up**
throw out the newspapers	**throw** them **out**

A. When is the repairman going to **bring back** our TV?

B. He's going to **bring** it **back** sometime next week.

1. When are you going to **call up** your uncle in Ohio?

2. When is Ted going to **throw out** his old newspapers?

3. When is your daughter going to **fill out** her college application forms?

4. When is Jeff going to **pick up** his clothes at the cleaner's?

5. When is Vicky going to **take back** her library books?

6. When are you going to **hook up** your new computer?

7. When is Howard going to **hang up** his new portrait?

8. When is Gloria going to **take down** her Christmas decorations?

9. When is Mr. Grumpkin going to **turn on** the heat in the building?

Oh, No! I Forgot!

> **put on** your boots
> **put** your boots **on**
>
> **put** them **on**

A. Did you remember to **turn off** the oven / **turn** the oven **off**?

B. Oh, no! I forgot! I'll **turn** it **off** right away.

1. *take back*
videos

2. *fill out*
the accident report

3. *turn on*
the alarm

4. *put away*
your toys

5. *hand in*
your English homework

6. *wake up*
the kids

7. *put on*
your raincoat

8. *take off*
your boots

9. *take out*
the garbage

How to Say It!

Remembering & Forgetting

A. Did you remember to *turn off the oven*?

B. Oh, no!
- I forgot!
- I forgot all about it!
- I completely forgot!
- It slipped my mind!
- It completely slipped my mind!

Practice the conversations in this lesson again. Tell that you forgot in different ways.

A BUSY SATURDAY

Everybody in the Peterson family is very busy today. It's Saturday, and they all have to do the things they didn't do during the week.

Mr. Peterson has to fill out his income tax form. He didn't have time to fill it out during the week.

Mrs. Peterson has to pick up her clothes at the cleaner's. She was too busy to pick them up during the week.

Their son Steve has to take his library books back. He forgot to take them back during the week.

Their other son, Michael, has to throw out all the old newspapers in the garage. He didn't have time to throw them out during the week.

Their daughter Stacey has to hook up the new modem for her computer. She was too busy to hook it up during the week.

And their other daughter, Abigail, has to put her toys away. She didn't feel like putting them away during the week.

As you can see, everybody in the Peterson family is going to be very busy today.

 READING *CHECK-UP*

Q & A

You're inviting somebody in the Peterson family to do something with you. Using this model, create dialogs based on the story.

A. Would you like to *play tennis* with me this morning?
B. I'd like to, but I can't. I have to *fill out my income tax form.*
A. That's too bad.
B. I know, but I've really got to do it. I *didn't have time to fill it out during the week.*
A. Well, maybe some other time.

How About You?

What do YOU have to do on your next day off from work or school?

I Don't Think So

A. Do you think I should keep these old love letters?

B. No, I don't think so. I think you should **throw** them **away**.

1. *hand in my homework*
do over

2. *use up this old milk*
throw out

3. *erase all my mistakes*
cross out

4. *leave the air conditioner on*
turn off

5. *try to remember Amy's telephone number*
write down

6. *ask the teacher the definition of this word*
look up

7. *make my decision right away*
think over

8. *keep my ex-boyfriend's ring*
give back

9. *accept this invitation to my ex-girlfriend's wedding*
turn down

LUCY'S ENGLISH COMPOSITION

Lucy is very discouraged. She handed in her English composition this morning, but her English teacher gave it back to her and told her to do it over. Apparently, her English teacher didn't like the way Lucy had done it. She hadn't erased her mistakes. She had simply crossed them out. Also, she had used several words incorrectly. She hadn't looked them up in a dictionary. And finally, she hadn't written her homework on the correct paper because she had accidentally thrown her notebook away. Poor Lucy! She didn't feel like writing her English composition in the first place, and now she has to do it over!

✔ READING *CHECK-UP*

TRUE, FALSE, OR MAYBE?

Answer True, False, or Maybe (if the answer isn't in the story).

1. Lucy gave her composition to her English teacher this morning.
2. Lucy's English teacher was satisfied with Lucy's composition.
3. The teacher gave back other students' compositions.
4. Lucy had made some mistakes in her composition.
5. Lucy knew the definitions of all the words she used in her composition.
6. Lucy is going to hand in her composition again tomorrow.

WHAT'S THE WORD?

Choose the correct words to complete the sentences.

cross __ out   do __ over   give __ back   hand __ in   look __ up   throw __ away

1. I need the dictionary you borrowed from me. Please _____.
2. I want to check your homework. Please _____.
3. Ms. Smith, there are too many mistakes in this letter. Please _____.
4. I haven't read today's newspaper yet. Please don't _____.
5. I don't remember his phone number. I've got to _____.
6. You should erase your mistakes. Don't just _____.

COMPLETE THE LETTERS

Complete these letters with the correct form of the verbs.

| call ___ up | give ___ back | think ___ over | throw ___ away | turn ___ down |

Dear Alice,

  I'm very discouraged. I'm having a lot of trouble with my girlfriend, and I don't know what to do. The problem is very simple. I'm in love with her, but she isn't in love with me. A few weeks ago, I gave her a ring, but she _____ **1** to me. During the past few months, I have written several love letters to her, but she has _____ **2**. Recently I asked her to marry me. She _____ **3** for a while, and then she _____ **4**. Now when I try to _____ **5**, she doesn't even want to talk to me. Please help me! I don't know what to do.

  "Discouraged Donald"
  Denver, Colorado

| hang ___ up | put ___ away | take ___ down | take ___ out | turn ___ off | turn ___ on |

Dear Alice,

  I'm extremely frustrated. My husband is a very difficult person. Every time I do something, he does the opposite. For example, every time I turn on the stereo system to listen to music, he _____ **1**. Every time I turn off the air conditioner in our apartment, he _____ **2**. Last week I bought a beautiful new painting for our bedroom. The day after I _____ **3**, he _____ **4**. We had a lot of old photographs on a table in our living room. I decided to _____ **5** in a closet, but two hours later he _____ **6**. Please help me! I don't know what to do.

  "Frustrated Fran"
  Phoenix, Arizona

What should "Discouraged Donald" and "Frustrated Fran" do? Write answers to their letters.

Would You Like to Get Together Today?

take back my library books = take my library books back

☑ **take** my library books **back**
☑ **pick up** my car at the repair shop
☑ **drop** my sister **off** at the airport

A. Would you like to get together today?

B. I'm afraid I can't. I have to **take** my library books **back**.

A. Are you free after you **take** them **back**?

B. I'm afraid not. I also have to **pick up** my car at the repair shop.

A. Would you like to get together after you **pick** it **up**?

B. I'd really like to, but I can't. I ALSO have to **drop** my sister **off** at the airport.

A. You're really busy today! What do you have to do after you **drop** her **off**?

B. Nothing. But by then I'll probably be exhausted. Let's get together tomorrow instead.

A. Fine. I'll call you in the morning.

A. Would you like to get together today?

B. I'm afraid I can't. I have to _____.

A. Are you free after you _____?

B. I'm afraid not. I also have to _____.

A. Would you like to get together after you _____?

B. I'd really like to, but I can't. I ALSO have to _____.

A. You're really busy today! What do you have to do after you _____?

B. Nothing. But by then I'll probably be exhausted. Let's get together tomorrow instead.

A. Fine. I'll call you in the morning.

1.
- ☑ **clean up** my living room
- ☑ **throw out** all my old newspapers
- ☑ **pick** my brother **up** at the train station

2.
- ☑ **figure out** my hospital bill
- ☑ **fill out** my insurance form
- ☑ **call** the doctor **up**

3.
- ☑ **take down** my Christmas decorations
- ☑ **hang up** my New Year's decorations
- ☑ **drop** my suit **off** at the cleaner's

4.
- ☑ **pick out** my wedding dress
- ☑ **write down** the names of all the wedding guests
- ☑ **pick** the wedding invitations **up**

5.
- ☑ **clean up** my room
- ☑ **put** my toys **away**
- ☑ **do** my math homework **over**

6.
- ☑ _____
- ☑ _____
- ☑ _____

I Heard from Her Just Last Week

hear from Aunt Betty	hear from her
~~hear Aunt Betty from~~	~~hear her from~~

A. Have you **heard from** Aunt Betty recently?

B. Yes, I have. I **heard from** her just last week.

1. Have you **run into** Mr. Clark recently?

2. Have you **run out of** paper recently?

3. Has Martha **gotten over** the flu yet?

4. Has your English teacher **called on** you recently?

5. Have you and your husband **looked through** your photo album recently?

6. Has Ricky been **picking on** his little sister recently?

How About You?

Tell about some of the people in your life.
   Do you have a good friend in another city? Who is he/she?
   How often do you hear from him/her? How long have you
      known each other?
   Who do you get along with very well? Why?
   Who do you take after? How?
   Who do you look up to? Why?

READING

A CHILD-REARING PROBLEM

Timothy and his little sister, Patty, don't get along with each other very well. In fact, they fight constantly. He picks on her when it's time for her to go to bed. She picks on him when his friends come over to play.

Timmy and Patty's parents are very concerned. They don't know what to do about their children. They have looked through several books on child rearing, but so far they can't seem to find an answer to the problem. They're hoping that eventually their children will learn to get along with each other better.

✔ READING CHECK-UP

TRUE, FALSE, OR MAYBE?

Answer True, False, or Maybe (if the answer isn't in the story).

1. Patty picks on Timmy when it's time for her go to bed.
2. Timmy is Patty's older brother.
3. Timmy and Patty's parents have a child-rearing problem.
4. They can't seem to find any books about child rearing.
5. Timmy and Patty will eventually learn to get along with each other better.

CHOOSE

1. Please don't _____ your little sister.
   a. pick on
   b. get along with

2. We've been _____ these old family pictures.
   a. looking through
   b. taking after

3. My history teacher _____ me three times today.
   a. looked up to
   b. called on

4. I haven't _____ my aunt and uncle recently.
   a. gotten over
   b. heard from

5. Everybody thinks I _____ my mother.
   a. take after
   b. look through

6. I really _____ my older sister because she's so smart.
   a. run into
   b. look up to

7. I _____ my cousin Jane on Main Street yesterday.
   a. ran into
   b. heard from

8. Don't kiss me! I haven't _____ my cold yet.
   a. gotten along with
   b. gotten over

ROLE PLAY *May I Help You?*

You're looking for clothing in a department store. Complete this conversation and act it out with another student.

A. May I help you?

B. Yes, please. I'm **looking for** (a / an) _____ .

A. What size do you wear?

B. $\begin{cases} \text{Size 32 / 34 / 36 / . . .} \\ \text{Small / Medium / Large / Extra Large.} \end{cases}$

A. Here. How do you like (this one / these)?

B. Hmm. I think (it's / they're) a little too _____ .* Do you have any _____ s that are a little _____ er?*

A. Yes. We have a wide selection. Why don't you **look through** all of our _____ s and **pick out** the (one / ones) you like?

B. Can I **try** (it / them) **on**?

A. Of course. You can **try** (it / them) **on** in the dressing room over there.

* fancy – plain
dark – light

[5 minutes later]

A. Well, how (does it / do they) fit?

B. I'm afraid (it's / they're) a little too _____.* Do you have any _____s that are a little _____er*?

A. Yes, we do. I think you'll like (THIS / THESE) _____. (It's / They're) a little _____er* than the one(s) you just **tried on**.

B. Will you **take** (it / them) **back** if I decide to return (it / them)?

A. Of course. No problem at all. Just **bring** (it / them) **back** within _____ days, and we'll **give** you your money **back**.

B. Fine. I think I'll take (it / them). How much (does it / do they) cost?

A. The usual price is _____ dollars. But you're in luck! We're having a sale this week, and all of our _____s are _____ percent off the regular price.

B. That's a real bargain! I'm glad I decided to buy (a / an) _____ this week. Thanks for your help.

* large – small
  long – short
  wide – narrow
  tight – loose (baggy)

1. *suit*   2. *jeans*   3. *sweater*   4.

How About You?

Where do you shop for clothing?
What kind of clothing do you like to wear?

Think about clothing you own:
    What's your favorite clothing item?
    How long have you had it?
    Where did you get it?
    Why is it your favorite?

ON SALE

Gary went to a men's clothing store yesterday. He was looking for a new sports jacket. He looked through the entire selection of jackets and picked out a few that he really liked. First, he picked out a nice blue jacket. But when he tried it on, it was too small. Next, he picked out an attractive red jacket. But when he tried it on, it was too large. Finally, he picked out a very fancy brown jacket with gold buttons. And when he tried it on, it seemed to fit perfectly.

Then he decided to buy a pair of trousers to go with the jacket. He looked through the entire selection of trousers and picked out several pairs that he really liked. First, he picked out a light brown pair. But when he tried them on, they were too tight. Next, he tried on a dark brown pair. But when he tried them on, they were too loose. Finally, he picked out a pair of brown-and-white plaid pants. And when he tried them on, they seemed to fit perfectly.

Gary paid for his new clothing and walked home feeling very happy about the jacket and pants he had just bought. He was especially happy because the clothing was on sale, and he had paid fifty percent off the regular price. However, Gary's happiness didn't last very long. When he got home, he noticed that one arm of the jacket was longer than the other. He also realized very quickly that the zipper on the pants was broken.

The next day Gary took the clothing back to the store and tried to get a refund. However, the people at the store refused to give him his money back because the clothing was on sale and there was a sign that said "All Sales Are Final!" Gary was furious, but he knew he couldn't do anything about it. The next time he buys something on sale, he'll be more careful. And he'll be sure to read the signs!

 READING *CHECK-UP*

WHAT'S THE SEQUENCE?

Put these events in the correct order, based on the story.

____ Gary picked out a few jackets he really liked.
____ Gary went back and asked for a refund.
_1_ Gary went shopping for clothes yesterday.
____ He walked home feeling very happy.
____ He walked home feeling very upset and angry.
____ The brown jacket seemed to fit perfectly.
____ The store refused to give him back his money.
____ A pair of plaid pants fit very well.
____ He paid only half of the regular price.
____ He picked out several pairs of trousers.
____ But then, Gary noticed a few problems with the jacket and the pants.

How About You?

Have you ever bought something you had to return?
 What did you buy?
 Where?
 What was wrong with it?
 What did you do?
 Were you successful?

LISTENING

Listen and choose what the people are talking about.

1. a. shorts
   b. a blouse

2. a. shoes
   b. a library book

3. a. an application form
   b. a math problem

4. a. homework
   b. children

5. a. pictures
   b. pants

6. a. the flu
   b. a decision

7. a. a coat
   b. the heat

8. a. milk
   b. the garbage

9. a. a telephone number
   b. an invitation

Listen. Then say it.

Turn it on!

Turn it off!

Clean it up!

Throw it away!

Say it. Then listen.

Fill it out!

Do it over!

Drop it off!

Hand it in!

Write in your journal about someone you look up to—a member of your family, a person in your community, or a famous person in your country or in history. Who do you look up to? Why do you admire this person?

CHAPTER SUMMARY

GRAMMAR

TWO-WORD VERBS: SEPARABLE

I'm going to	**put on** my boots. **put** my boots **on**. **put** them **on**.

TWO-WORD VERBS: INSEPARABLE

I	**hear from** Aunt Betty **hear from** her ~~hear Aunt Betty from~~ ~~hear her from~~	very often.

KEY VOCABULARY

TWO-WORD VERBS: SEPARABLE

bring __ back	give __ back	put __ away	throw __ out
call __ up	hand __ in	put __ on	try __ on
clean __ up	hang __ up	take __ back	turn __ down
cross __ out	hook __ up	take __ down	turn __ off
do __ over	leave __ on	take __ off	turn __ on
drop __ off	look __ up	take __ out	use __ up
figure __ out	pick __ out	think __ over	wake __ up
fill __ out	pick __ up	throw __ away	write __ down

TWO-WORD VERBS: INSEPARABLE

call on	look through
come over	look up to
get along with	pick on
get over	run into
hear from	run out of
look for	take after

10

Connectors:
And . . . Too
And . . . Either
So, But, Neither

- Coincidences
- Asking for and Giving Reasons
- Describing People's Backgrounds, Interests, and Personalities
- Looking for a Job
- Referring People to Someone Else
- Discussing Opinions
- Describing People's Similarities and Differences

VOCABULARY PREVIEW

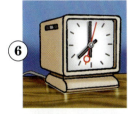

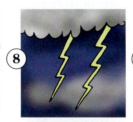
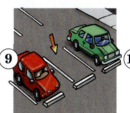

1. allergic
2. athletic
3. frightened
4. strict
5. lenient
6. alarm clock
7. army
8. lightning
9. parking space
10. want ad
11. enroll
12. hide
13. kiss
14. walk *my* dog
15. work out

What a Coincidence!

I'm hungry.	{ I am, too. So am I. }		
I can swim.	{ I can, too. So can I. }	I have a car.	{ I do, too. So do I. }
I've seen that movie.	{ I have, too. So have I. }	I worked yesterday.	{ I did, too. So did I. }

A. I'm allergic to cats.

B. What a coincidence!
{ I am, too.
So am I. }

1. I'm a vegetarian.

2. I like peppermint ice cream.

3. I can speak four languages fluently.

4. I just got a raise.

5. I'll be on a business trip next week.

6. I've been feeling tired lately.

7. I have to work late at the office tonight.

8. I forgot my umbrella this morning.

9.

What a Coincidence!

I'm not hungry.	{ I'm not either. / Neither am I. }
I can't swim.	{ I can't either. / Neither can I. }
I haven't seen that movie.	{ I haven't either. / Neither have I. }

I don't have a car.	{ I don't either. / Neither do I. }
I didn't work yesterday.	{ I didn't either. / Neither did I. }

A. I'm not a very good dancer.

B. What a coincidence!
{ I'm not either. / Neither am I. }

1. I don't like macaroni and cheese.

2. I didn't see the stop sign.

3. I can't skate very well.

4. I haven't seen a movie in a long time.

5. I wasn't very athletic when I was younger.

6. I won't be able to go bowling next Saturday.

7. I don't have a date for the prom.

8. I've never kissed anyone before.

9.

And They Do, Too

I'm tired, { and he is, too. / and so is he. }

He'll be busy, { and she will, too. / and so will she. }

She's been sick, { and he has, too. / and so has he. }

They sing, { and she does, too. / and so does she. }

She studied, { and I did, too. / and so did I. }

A. Why can't you or the children help me with the dishes?

B. I have to study, { **and they do, too.** / **and so do they.** }

1. Why weren't you and Bob at the meeting this morning?

I missed the bus, _____.

2. Why are you and Vanessa so nervous today?

I have two final exams tomorrow, _____.

3. What are you and your brother going to do when you grow up?

I'm going to start an Internet company, _____.

4. Where were you and your wife when the accident happened?

I was standing on the corner, _____.

5. How do you know Mr. and Mrs. Crandall?

They walk their dog in the park, _____.

6. Why can't you or your roommates come to my party?

I'll be out of town, _____.

7. Why haven't you and your brother been in school for the past few days?

I've been sick, _____.

8. Could you or your friend help me take these packages upstairs?

I'll be glad to help you, _____.

9. How did you meet your wife?

I was working out at the health club, _____.

10. What are you two arguing about?

He wants this parking space, _____.

11. Why don't you or your neighbors complain about this leak?

I've already spoken to the landlord, _____.

12. How did you and your husband like the play?

I fell asleep during the first act, _____.

13. Why are you and your cats hiding under the bed?

I'm afraid of thunder and lightning, _____.

14.

"MADE FOR EACH OTHER"

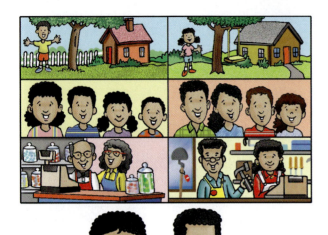

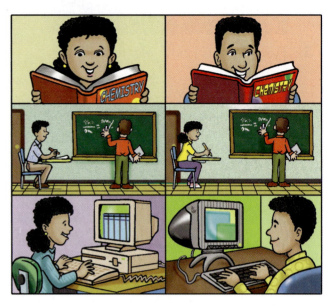

Louise and Brian are very compatible people. They have a lot in common. For example, they have similar backgrounds. He grew up in a small town in the South, and so did she. She's the oldest of four children, and he is, too. His parents own their own business, and so do hers.

They also have similar academic interests. She's majoring in chemistry, and he is, too. He has taken every course in mathematics offered by their college, and so has she. She enjoys working with computers, and he does, too.

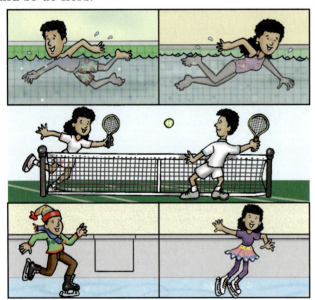

In addition, Louise and Brian like the same sports. He goes swimming several times a week, and so does she. She can play tennis very well, and so can he. His favorite winter sport is ice skating, and hers is, too.

Louise and Brian also have the same cultural interests. She has been to most of the art museums in New York City, and so has he. He's a member of the college theater group, and she is, too. She has a complete collection of Beethoven's symphonies, and so does he.

In addition, they have similar personalities. She has always been very shy, and he has, too. He tends to be very quiet, and so does she. She's often nervous when she's in large groups of people, and he is, too.

Finally, they have very similar outlooks on life. She has been a vegetarian for years, and so has he. He supports equal rights for women and minorities, and so does she. She's opposed to the use of nuclear energy, and he is, too.

As you can see, Louise and Brian are very compatible people. In fact, everybody says they were "made for each other."

 ## READING *CHECK-UP*

TRUE, FALSE, OR MAYBE?

Answer True, False, or Maybe (if the answer isn't in the story).

1. Louise spent her childhood in the South.
2. Brian has older brothers and sisters.
3. Louise and Brian are both students in college.
4. They both ski very well.
5. They haven't been to all the art museums in New York City.
6. They both like to be in large groups of people.
7. They both feel that people shouldn't eat vegetables.

LISTENING

Listen and choose what the people are talking about.

1. a. personality
   b. background

2. a. sports
   b. cultural interests

3. a. academic interests
   b. outlook on life

4. a. personality
   b. background

5. a. sports
   b. academic interests

6. a. cultural interests
   b. outlook on life

And She Hasn't Either

I'm not tired, { and he isn't either. / and neither is he. }

He won't be busy, { and she won't either. / and neither will she. }

She hasn't been sick, { and he hasn't either. / and neither has he. }

They don't sing, { and she doesn't either. / and neither does she. }

She didn't study, { and I didn't either. / and neither did I. }

A. Why do you and your sister look so frightened?

B. I've never been on a roller coaster before, { **and she hasn't either.** / **and neither has she.** }

1. Why haven't you and your roommate hooked up your new DVD player?
   I don't understand the instructions, _____.

2. Why didn't you or your parents answer the telephone all weekend?
   I wasn't home, _____.

3. Why did you and your wife move to the center of the city?
   She didn't like living in the suburbs, _____.

4. What do you and Greg want to talk to me about?
   I won't be able to work overtime this weekend, _____.

5. Why do you and your husband want to enroll in my dance class?

I don't know how to dance, ____.

6. Why does the school nurse want to see us?

I haven't had an eye examination, ____.

7. Why didn't you or Mom wake us up on time this morning?

I didn't hear the alarm clock, ____.

8. Why did you and your husband leave the concert so early?

I couldn't stand the loud music, ____.

9. What are you and your sister arguing about?

She doesn't want to take the garbage out, ____.

10. Why don't you and your friends want to come to the game?

They aren't very interested in football, ____.

11. Why were you and your wife so nervous during the flight?

I had never flown before today, ____.

12. Why have you and your friends stopped shopping at my store?

I can't afford your prices, ____.

13. Why don't you and your sister want me to read "Little Red Riding Hood"?

I don't like fairy tales very much, ____.

14.

LAID OFF

Jack and Betty Williams are going through some difficult times. They were both laid off from their jobs last month. As the days go by, they're becoming more and more concerned about their futures, since he hasn't been able to find another job yet, and neither has she.

The layoffs weren't a surprise to Jack and Betty. After all, Jack's company hadn't been doing very well for a long time, and neither had Betty's. However, Jack had never expected both of them to be laid off at the same time, and Betty hadn't either. Ever since they have been laid off, Jack and Betty have been trying to find new jobs. Unfortunately, she hasn't been very successful, and he hasn't either.

The main reason they're having trouble finding work is that there simply aren't many jobs available right now. He can't find anything in the want ads, and neither can she. She hasn't heard about any job openings, and he hasn't either. His friends haven't been able to help at all, and neither have hers.

Another reason they're having trouble finding work is that they don't seem to have the right kind of skills and training. He doesn't know anything about computers, and she doesn't either. She can't type very well, and neither can he. He hasn't had any special vocational training, and she hasn't either.

A third reason they're having trouble finding work is that there are certain jobs they prefer not to take. He doesn't like working at night, and neither does she. She isn't willing to work on the weekends, and neither is he. He doesn't want to commute very far to work, and she doesn't either.

Despite all their problems, Jack and Betty aren't completely discouraged. She doesn't have a very pessimistic outlook on life, and neither does he. They're both hopeful that things will get better soon.

 READING *CHECK-UP*

TRUE, FALSE, OR MAYBE?

Answer True, False, or Maybe (if the answer isn't in the story).

1. Betty quit her job last month.
2. Jack and Betty had been working for the same company.
3. Some of their friends have been laid off, too.
4. Typing skills are important in certain jobs.
5. Jack and Betty will find jobs soon.

A Job Interview

You're at a job interview. Role-play with another student, using the interviewer's questions below.

Tell me about your skills.
Tell me about your educational background.
Have you had any special vocational training?
Are you willing to work at night or on the weekend?
When can you start?

You Should Ask Them

I don't sing, **but** my sister does.
She didn't know the answer, **but** I did.

He can play chess, **but** I can't.
We're ready, **but** they aren't.

A. Can you baby-sit for us tomorrow night?

B. No, I can't, but my SISTER can. You should ask HER.

1. Have you heard the weather forecast?
my father

2. Do you have a hammer?
my upstairs neighbors

3. Are you interested in seeing a movie tonight?
Maria

4. Did you write down the homework assignment?
Jack

5. Have you by any chance found a brown-and-white dog?
the woman across the street

6. Were you paying attention when the salesman explained how to assemble this?
the children

How to Say It!

Offering a Suggestion

You should *ask HER.*

Why don't you *ask HER?*

How about *asking HER?*

Practice the conversations in this lesson again. Offer suggestions in different ways.

"TOUCHY SUBJECTS"

Larry and his parents always disagree when they talk about politics. Larry is very liberal, but his parents aren't. They're very conservative. Larry thinks the president is doing a very poor job, but his parents don't. They think the president is doing a fine job. Also, Larry doesn't think the government should spend a lot of money on defense, but his parents do. They think the country needs a strong army. You can see why Larry and his parents always disagree when they talk about politics. Politics is a very "touchy subject" with them.

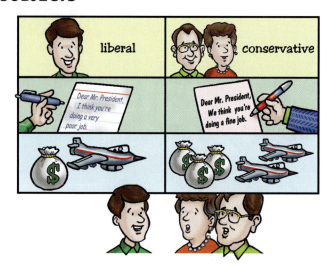

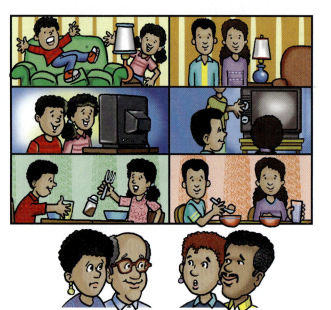

The Greens and their next-door neighbors, the Harrisons, always disagree when they talk about child rearing. The Greens are very lenient with their children, but the Harrisons aren't. They're very strict. The Greens let their children watch television whenever they want, but the Harrisons don't. They let their children watch television for only an hour a day. Also, the Harrisons have always taught their children to sit quietly and behave well at the dinner table, but the Greens haven't. They have always allowed their children to do whatever they want at the dinner table. You can see why the Greens and the Harrisons always disagree when they talk about child rearing. Child rearing is a very "touchy subject" with them.

 ## ✔ READING *CHECK-UP*

TRUE, FALSE, OR MAYBE?

Answer True, False, or Maybe (if the answer isn't in the story).

1. Larry and his parents never agree when they talk about politics.
2. Larry probably supports equal rights for women and minorities.
3. The Harrisons' children watch television more often than the Greens' children.
4. The Greens' children probably go to bed later than the Harrisons' children.
5. Since the Greens and the Harrisons disagree, they never talk about child rearing.

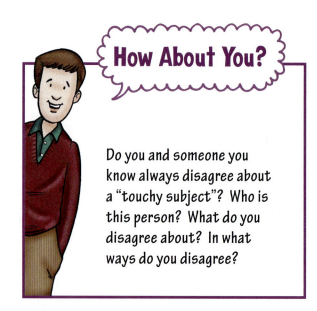

How About You?

Do you and someone you know always disagree about a "touchy subject"? Who is this person? What do you disagree about? In what ways do you disagree?

In many ways, my sister and I are exactly the same.
    I'm tall and thin, and she is, too.
    I have brown eyes and curly black hair, and so does she.
    I work in an office downtown, and she does, too.
    I'm not married yet, and neither is she.
    I went to college in Boston, and so did she.
    I wasn't a very good student, and she wasn't either.

And in many ways, my sister and I are very different.
    I like classical music, but she doesn't.
    She enjoys sports, but I don't.
    I've never traveled overseas, but she has.
    She's never been to New York, but I have many times.
    She's very outgoing and popular, but I'm not.
    I'm very quiet and philosophical, but she isn't.

Yes, in many ways, my sister and I are exactly the same, and in many ways, we're very different. But most important of all, we like and respect each other. And we're friends.

Tell other students about somebody you are close to—a friend, a classmate, or someone in your family. Tell how you and this person are the same, and tell how you are different.

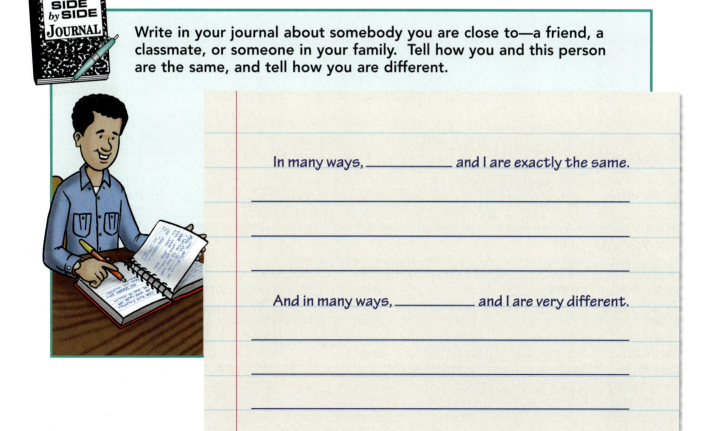

Write in your journal about somebody you are close to—a friend, a classmate, or someone in your family. Tell how you and this person are the same, and tell how you are different.

In many ways, _____ and I are exactly the same.

_____

_____

_____

And in many ways, _____ and I are very different.

_____

_____

_____

Listen. Then say it.

No, I can't, but my SISTER can.

No, I don't, but my NEIGHBORS do.

You should ask HER.

Why don't you ask THEM?

Say it. Then listen.

No, I haven't, but my FATHER has.

No, I wasn't, but my CHILDREN were.

You should ask HIM.

How about asking THEM?

CHAPTER SUMMARY

GRAMMAR

CONNECTORS:

TOO/SO

I'm hungry.	I am, too. So am I.
I can swim.	I can, too. So can I.
I've seen that movie.	I have, too. So have I.
I have a car.	I do, too. So do I.
I worked yesterday.	I did, too. So did I.

EITHER/NEITHER

I'm not hungry.	I'm not either. Neither am I.
I can't swim.	I can't either. Neither can I.
I've haven't seen that movie.	I haven't either. Neither have I.
I don't have a car.	I don't either. Neither do I.
I didn't work.	I didn't either. Neither did I.

BUT

I don't sing, **but** my sister does.
She didn't know the answer, **but** I did.
He can play chess, **but** I can't.
We're ready, **but** they aren't.

I'm tired,	and he is, too. and so is he.
He'll be busy,	and she will, too. and so will she.
She's been sick,	and he has, too. and so has he.
They sing,	and she does, too. and so does she.
She studied,	and I did, too. and so did I.

I'm not tired,	and he isn't either. and neither is he.
He won't be busy,	and she won't either. and neither will she.
She hasn't been sick,	and he hasn't either. and neither has he.
They don't sing,	and she doesn't either. and neither does she.
She didn't study,	and I didn't either. and neither did I.

KEY VOCABULARY

DESCRIBING

academic
allergic
athletic
available
compatible
concerned
conservative
cultural
discouraged
frightened
hopeful
lenient
liberal
pessimistic
philosophical
similar
strict
willing

PEOPLE AND THINGS

act
alarm clock
army
art museum
background
business trip
child rearing
collection
defense
equal rights
fairy tale
final exam
government
job opening
layoff
leak
lightning
minorities
nuclear energy
outlook on life
parking space
personality
raise
theater group
thunder
training
vegetarian
vocational
    training
want ads

ACTIONS

afford
allow
behave
commute
enroll
expect
hide
kiss
major in
prefer
respect
support
tend to
walk *my*
    dog
work out

Feature Article
Fact File
Around the World
Interview
We've Got Mail!

Global Exchange
Listening
Fun with Idioms
What Are They
Saying?

Volume 3   Number 4

From Matchmakers to Dating Services

Traditions, customs, modern life, and the ways people meet

Marriage traditions and customs are very different around the world. In many cultures, young people meet at school, at work, or in other places; they decide to go out together; they fall in love; and they get married. In other cultures, parents or other family members arrange a match between two young people.

In India, for example, a father traditionally finds his daughter a husband. The father might ask friends or relatives to recommend a possible husband, and he might put an ad in the newspaper. The father looks for someone with a good education, occupation, and salary. When he finds a possible match, he sends his daughter's horoscope to the boy's family. An astrologer reads the horoscope and decides if there is a good astrological match between the young man and woman. If the astrologer approves, the families then discuss the marriage arrangements.

In many cultures around the world, families use a matchmaker to bring young people together and arrange marriages. This is especially common in rural areas of many countries. Families pay the matchmaker to find a partner for their child. Sometimes, the matchmaker also helps families with the "business" part of a marriage agreement. For example, a family may give or receive animals, products, or other valuable things as part of the marriage arrangement. In some cultures, parents even arrange marriages between children before they are born.

An astrologer approved the marriage of these newlyweds from India. The astrologer examined their horoscopes to decide if the date and time of their births were a good match.

These traditions and customs are changing in many places, especially in the modern cities of the world. Young people want the freedom to choose their own partners. Many, however, actually use modern-day versions of the traditional matchmaking services! For example, some people put personal ads in newspapers or magazines. In these ads, people describe themselves and tell what kind of person they're looking for. Others use dating services—companies that bring people together. Most dating services ask people to submit a photograph and fill out a long questionnaire about their background and interests. Some dating services even make videos of their customers. People who use a dating service can usually browse through the company's information to find a possible partner.

FACT FILE

When People Get Married

People around the world get married at different ages. At what age do men and women usually get married in different countries you know?

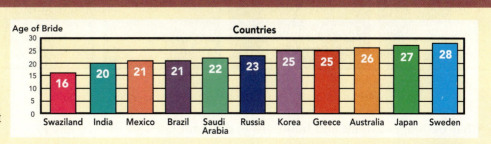

Age of Bride   Countries

Swaziland	India	Mexico	Brazil	Saudi Arabia	Russia	Korea	Greece	Australia	Japan	Sweden
16	20	21	21	22	23	25	25	26	27	28

Wedding Customs and Traditions

a wedding ceremony in the United States

a Hindu ceremony

a wedding in the Slovak Republic

a ceremony in a Korean village

Wedding customs and traditions are very different around the world. In many cultures, weddings happen in churches or other places of worship. In other cultures, people get married outdoors, in their homes, in special reception halls for family celebrations, or in other places. The bride and the groom usually wear clothing that is traditional for weddings in their culture. The type of clothing and the colors are very different around the world. Brides often wear a veil or a crown on their heads. Some weddings are private—just for family members and friends. Other weddings are public. Everybody in the neighborhood or the entire town might attend the celebration. Some weddings are short, and other weddings can last for hours, days, or even a week!

a traditional Romanian dance

musicians leading a wedding procession

Music and dancing are an important part of wedding celebrations in different cultures. There are often special dances for the bride and groom, their parents, and other family members. Musicians might play special wedding music during the ceremony, at the celebration after the ceremony, or even in the street!

confetti

flower petals

rice

In some cultures, people like to throw things at weddings! Before or after the ceremony, it is often traditional for guests to shower the bride and groom with something to wish them good luck.

Guests have pinned money on this bride and groom in Cyprus.

a wedding couple in Colombia lighting candles during the ceremony

cutting the cake at a U.S. wedding celebration

a Japanese bride arriving at her wedding by boat

a bride in the U.S. throwing a bouquet of flowers (According to tradition, the person who catches it will get married next.)

Many cultures around the world have special wedding customs. These traditions often involve candles, flowers, special foods, money, and the ways that couples get to their wedding ceremonies.

What wedding customs and traditions in different cultures do you know?

Interview

A *Side by Side Gazette* reporter spoke with several young couples.

Q: "How did you meet?"

A: We met in college.

A: We met at work.

A: We met at a bookstore.

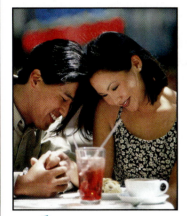

A: We were high school "sweethearts."

A: We met on a "blind date" that our friends arranged.

A: We met through a dating service.

A: Our parents arranged our marriage through a matchmaker.

FUN with IDIOMS

He's nuts about me.

She gave me the cold shoulder.

I fell for him the moment I met him.

We had planned to go on a date, but she stood me up.

Do You Know These Expressions?

_____ 1. He's nuts about me.

_____ 2. She gave me the cold shoulder.

_____ 3. I fell for him the moment I met him.

_____ 4. We had planned to go on a date, but she stood me up.

a. I liked him right away.

b. He likes me a lot.

c. She didn't meet me.

d. She didn't pay attention to me.

We've Got Mail!

Dear Side by Side,

  I'm trying to figure out two-word verbs. Is there a rule that will tell me which two-word verbs are separable and which are inseparable? I hope to hear you from soon.

    Sincerely,

      "Looking for an Answer"

Dear "Looking for an Answer,"

  We're sorry to tell you that there isn't a rule for this. You need to learn about each verb separately. Here's a suggestion. On a piece of paper, make two lists. Write down separable two-word verbs in one list and inseparable two-word verbs in the other. Then look up the words on your lists when you can't remember them.

  By the way, we've circled some words in the last sentence of your letter because "hear from" is an inseparable two-word verb. The correct way to say this is "I hope to hear from you soon." Thanks for writing, and good luck with two-word verbs!

    Sincerely,

      Side by Side

Dear Side by Side,

  I think two-word verbs are very difficult. The verb in a two-word verb has one meaning, but the whole two-word verb often has a different meaning. For example, "I turned on the light," but "I turned down the invitation"; "I take out the garbage," but "I take after my father." In my language, we have different words for all these expressions. Why does English use the same words over and over again?

    Sincerely,

      "Turned Off by Two-Word Verbs"

Dear "Turned Off,"

  We're sorry to hear you're unhappy. Two-word verbs are very common in everyday English. We actually have special words for many of these meanings, but these words are more formal. For example, you can say, "I declined the invitation" and "I resemble my father." Most English speakers, however, prefer to use informal language, so they use lots of two-word verbs. With time, we're sure you'll get over this problem with two-word verbs. Thanks for your question.

    Sincerely,

      Side by Side

Global Exchange

PedroJ: Let me tell you about my best friend. His name is Marco. People think we're brothers because we look alike. He's short and thin, and so am I. I have curly brown hair, and he does, too. We also have similar backgrounds. He's originally from Peru, and I am, too. He moved to this country when he was a little boy, and so did I. His parents work in factories, and so do mine. Marco and I have very different interests. He enjoys playing sports, but I don't. I play a musical instrument, but he doesn't. I've been in several plays in school, but he hasn't. How about you? Tell me about your best friend.

Tell a keypal about your best friend.

LISTENING

"Telephone Tag" True or False?

True!

_____ ❶ Mary likes jazz, and Jim does, too.

_____ ❷ Mary likes to play tennis, and so does Jim.

_____ ❸ Jim wants to go to the ballet, but Mary doesn't.

_____ ❹ Jim hasn't seen the movie, and neither has Mary.

_____ ❺ Jim doesn't like Italian food, but Mary does.

What Are They Saying?

HILL

Listening Scripts

Chapter 1 – Page 6

Listen and choose the correct answer.

1. What are you doing?
2. Do you watch the news very often?
3. Are you a good swimmer?
4. What's Cathy reading?
5. Who cooks in your family?
6. Do they like to skate?
7. Does your sister want to be a ballet dancer?
8. Do you and your friends play basketball very often?
9. Are your parents good dancers?
10. What does Peter want to be when he grows up?

Chapter 2 – Page 17

Listen and choose the correct answer.

1. Did you do well at your job interview yesterday?
2. Were your children tired last night?
3. What was he doing when he broke his leg?
4. Did you finish your dinner last night?
5. How did your husband lose his wallet?
6. What was your supervisor doing?
7. Did you do well on the exam?
8. What happened while you were preparing lunch?

Chapter 3 – Page 24

Listen to the conversation and choose the answer that is true.

1. A. Are you going to wear your brown suit today?
   B. No, I don't think so. I wore my brown suit yesterday. I'm going to wear my gray suit.
2. A. Let's make beef stew for dinner!
   B. But we had that last week. Let's make spaghetti and meatballs instead.
   A. Okay.
3. A. Do you want to watch the game show on Channel 5 or the news program on Channel 9?
   B. Let's watch the news program.
4. A. What's the matter with it?
   B. The brakes don't work, and it doesn't start very well in the morning.
5. A. What are you going to do tomorrow?
   B. I'm going to plant carrots, tomatoes, and lettuce.
6. A. This computer is very powerful, but it's too expensive.
   B. You're right.

Side by Side Gazette – Page 35

Listen to the messages on Dave's machine. Match the messages.

You have five messages.

Message Number One: "Hi, Dave. It's Sarah. Thanks for the invitation, but I can't come to your party tomorrow. I'll be taking my uncle to the hospital. Maybe next time." [*beep*]

Message Number Two: "Hello, Dave. It's Bob. I'm sorry that my wife and I won't be able to come to your party tomorrow. We'll be attending a wedding out of town. I hope it's a great party. Have fun!" [*beep*]

Message Number Three: "Dave? It's Paula. How's it going? I got your message about the party tomorrow. Unfortunately, I won't be able to go. I'll be studying all weekend. Talk to you soon." [*beep*]

Message Number Four: "Hi, Dave. It's Joe. Thanks for the invitation to your party. I'll be visiting my parents in New York City, so I'm afraid I won't be around. I'll call you when I get back." [*beep*]

Message Number Five: "Hello, Dave? It's Carla. Thanks for the invitation to your party. I don't have anything to do tomorrow night, so I'll definitely be there. I'm really looking forward to it. See you tomorrow." [*beep*]

Chapter 4 – Page 49

1. *Linda is on vacation in San Francisco. This is her list of things to do. Check the things on the list Linda has already done.*

   Linda has already seen the Golden Gate Bridge. She hasn't visited Golden Gate Park yet. She took a tour of Alcatraz Prison yesterday. She's going to go to Chinatown tomorrow. She hasn't ridden a cable car yet. She's eaten at Fisherman's Wharf, but she hasn't had time to buy souvenirs.

2. *Alan is a secretary in a very busy office. This is his list of things to do before 5 P.M. on Friday. Check the things on the list Alan has already done.*

   Alan has already called Mrs. Porter. He has to type the letter to the Mervis Company. He hasn't taken the mail to the post office yet. He's gone to the bank. He hasn't sent an e-mail to the company's office in Denver, and he's going to speak to the boss about his salary next week.

3. *It's Saturday, and Judy and Paul Johnson are doing lots of things around the house. This is the list of things they have to do today. Check the things on the list they've already done.*

   Judy and Paul haven't done the laundry. They have to wash the kitchen windows. They've paid the bills. They haven't given the dog a bath. They'll clean the garage later. They couldn't fix the bathroom sink or repair the fence, but they vacuumed the living room rug.

Chapter 5 – Page 60

Listen to the conversation and choose the answer that is true.

1. A. How long have you had a backache?
   B. For three days.
2. A. Has your father always been an engineer?
   B. No, he hasn't.
3. A. How long has your knee been swollen?
   B. For a week.
4. A. How long have you known how to ski?
   B. Since I was a teenager.
5. A. Did you live in Tokyo for a long time?
   B. Yes. Five years.
6. A. How long has Roger been interested in Egyptian history?
   B. Since he lived in Cairo.
7. A. Is Amy still in the hospital?
   B. Oh. I forgot to tell you. She's been home for two days.
8. A. Have you played hockey for a long time?
   B. Yes. I've played hockey since I moved to Toronto three years ago.

Side by Side Gazette – Page 67

Listen to the voice-mail messages between Gloria Rivera and her office assistant, Sam. Has Sam done the things on Ms. Rivera's list? Check Yes or No.

You have one message. Tuesday, 8:15 A.M.

Hello, Sam? This is Ms. Rivera. I'll be out of the office all day today. I'm not feeling well. Here's a list of things you'll need to do while I'm not here. First, please write a note to Mrs. Wilson and tell her I'm sick. Then, please call Mr. Chen and change the time of our appointment. Also, send an e-mail to everybody in the office, and tell them about next week's meeting. Don't forget to speak to the custodian about my broken desk lamp. I hope he can fix it. Hmm. Let's see. I know there are a few more things. Oh, yes. Please make a list of all the employees and give it to Ms. Baxter. She asked me for the list last week. Okay, Sam. I think that's everything. Oh . . . one more thing. Please take the package on my desk to the post office if you have time. And that's it. Thanks, Sam. I'll see you tomorrow morning.

You have reached the voice mailbox of Gloria Rivera. Please leave a message after the tone.

Ms. Rivera? This is Sam. I'm sorry you aren't feeling well. I hope you feel better tomorrow. I'm calling to tell you what I've done today, and what I haven't done yet. It's been very busy here, so I haven't had time to do everything. I wrote a note to Mrs. Wilson. I called Mr. Chen and changed the time of your appointment. I also sent the e-mail about next week's meeting. I haven't spoken to the custodian. He's been sick all week. I made a list of all the employees, but I haven't given it to Ms. Baxter yet. I'll give it to her early tomorrow morning. Finally, I haven't taken the package to the post office yet. I haven't had time. I'm going to take it to the post office on my way home. Again, I hope you're feeling better. I'll see you in the morning.

Chapter 6 – Page 79

WHICH WORD DO YOU HEAR?

Listen and choose the correct answer.

1. He's gone to the bank.
2. I've never written so many letters in one day before.
3. She's been seeing patients all day.
4. What courses have you taken this year?
5. Is Beverly giving blood?
6. Ben has driven all night.

WHO IS SPEAKING?

Listen and decide who is speaking.

1. What a day! All the tenants have been complaining that nothing is working.
2. I'm very tired. I've given six lessons today.
3. Thank you! You've been a wonderful audience!
4. I'm really tired. I've been watching them all day.
5. I'm very tired. I've been looking at paychecks since early this morning.
6. It's been a long day. I've been selling tickets since ten A.M.

Chapter 7 – Page 93

Listen and choose the correct answer.

1. A. I avoid going to the mall whenever I can.
   B. Me, too.
2. A. I've decided to sell my car.
   B. Your beautiful car?
3. A. Please try to quit biting your nails.
   B. Okay. Mom.
4. A. Do you enjoy traveling by plane?
   B. Very much.
5. A. We're thinking about moving to Florida.
   B. Oh. That's interesting.
6. A. I've been considering getting married for a long time.
   B. Oh, really? I didn't know that.
7. A. Don't stop practicing.
   B. Okay.
8. A. Interrupting people is a habit I just can't break.
   B. That's too bad.

Chapter 8 – Page 103

Listen and choose the correct answer.

1. Did your parents enjoy eating at Joe's Restaurant last night?
2. Why don't you want to see the new James Bond movie with us next weekend?
3. Did you get to the play on time last night?
4. Michael, please go upstairs and do your homework.
5. Why did Carmen do so well on the history test?
6. We really enjoyed our vacation at the Ritz Hotel.

Side by Side Gazette – Page 113

Listen to the Olympic Game highlights. Match the highlight and the sport.

And now, sports fans, let's finish today's program with highlights of the Olympic Games. Here are five of my favorite moments in the most recent summer and winter games:

There are three seconds left in the game. Number 38 gets ready to shoot again. His team needs this point to win the game. He shoots, and it's in the basket! [Buzzer] That's it! The game is over! And the United States wins 99 to 98. The U.S. gets the gold medal!

Kirshner is still in front. But wait! Look at Tanaka in the next lane! What speed! Look at him move through the water! Tanaka is even with Kirshner. Now Tanaka is ahead! And Tanaka wins the event! Japan wins the gold medal, Germany gets the silver, and Hungary gets the bronze.

Natasha knows she must do this floor routine perfectly to win the gold medal. She had problems today when she fell off the balance beam, and that's usually her best event. She's doing very well. What a strong and graceful athlete! And here's the most difficult part of her routine. Beautiful! But, oh . . . she falls! Natasha has fallen at the very end of her routine. What a shame! There will be no gold for Natasha this year.

What a race! Anderson is still in first place and Sanchez is right behind him in second place. Look at Sanchez run! He's moving ahead of Anderson. The lead has changed! Sanchez is now in front! He crosses the finish line! Sanchez wins with a time of two hours, ten minutes, and eleven seconds. So Mexico wins the gold, Canada gets the silver, and France gets the bronze.

And Tamara leaves the ice after a beautiful long program! I think that's one of the best programs I've ever seen at the Olympics. She moved so gracefully to the music. Let's see what the judges think. Look at these marks! Five-point-eight, five-point-nine, five-point-nine, five-point-eight, five-point-seven, five-point-nine, five-point-nine, six-point-oh, five-point-eight. Excellent scores! Tamara wins the gold medal! Look at all the flowers people are throwing on the ice! I'm sure this is the happiest day of Tamara's life!

Chapter 9 – Page 129

Listen and choose what the people are talking about.

1. A. Where can I try them on?
   B. The dressing room is over there.

2. A. Now remember, you can't bring them back!
   B. I understand.

3. A. Have you filled it out yet?
   B. No. I'm having some trouble. Can you help me?

4. A. Please drop them off at the school by eight o'clock.
   B. By eight o'clock? Okay.

5. A. Where should I hang them?
   B. What about over the fireplace?

6. A. Have you thought it over?
   B. Yes, I have.

7. A. It's cold in here.
   B. You're right. I'll turn it on.

8. A. Should we use it up?
   B. No. Let's throw it out.

9. A. What are you going to do?
   B. I'm going to turn it down.

Chapter 10 – p. 137

Listen and choose what the people are talking about.

1. A. To tell the truth, I'm a little shy.
   B. What a coincidence! I am, too.

2. A. I enjoy going to plays and concerts.
   B. We're very compatible. So do I.

3. A. I'm enjoying this course.
   B. I am, too.

4. A. I'm from Minnesota.
   B. That's interesting. So am I.

5. A. I go swimming three times a week.
   B. What a coincidence! I do, too.

6. A. I'm opposed to using animals in scientific experiments.
   B. I am, too.

Side by Side Gazette – Page 148

Listen to the messages on Mary and Jim's answering machines. Answer true or false.

[Monday, 6:15 P.M.]

Hi, Mary. It's Jim. Are you by any chance interested in going to a jazz concert this Friday night? Please call me and let me know. Talk to you later.

[Monday, 9:13 P.M.]

Hi, Jim. It's Mary. I'm returning your call. Thanks for the invitation. I know you like jazz, and I do, too. And I'd really like to go to the concert with you, but I have to work this Friday night. Do you want to play tennis on Saturday afternoon? Let me know. 'Bye.

[Tuesday, 3:40 P.M.]

Hi, Mary. It's Jim. I'm sorry I missed your call last night. I was at the laundromat, and I got home very late. I'm free on Saturday, but unfortunately, I really don't like to play tennis. Actually, I'm a very bad tennis player. Do you want to go to the ballet with me on Saturday night? Let me know, and I'll order tickets. Talk to you soon.

[Wednesday, 5:50 P.M.]

Hi, Jim. It's Mary. I got your message. Believe it or not, I've already gone to the ballet this week. I went with my sister last night. I have an idea! Let's see the new Steven Steelberg movie. I hear that it's great. Call and let me know.

[Thursday, 6:30 P.M.]

Hi, Mary. It's Jim. Sorry I missed your call again. I guess we're playing "telephone tag!" The movie sounds great. I haven't seen it yet. Do you want to have dinner before the movie? There's a wonderful new Italian restaurant downtown. Let me know. 'Bye.

[Friday, 5:17 P.M.]

Hi, Jim. Guess who! You won't believe it! I just found out that I have to work this Saturday night. It's a shame because I really wanted to see that movie. I'm not busy on Sunday. Are you free on Sunday afternoon? Let me know. By the way, I don't really like Italian food very much. There's a very good Greek restaurant in my neighborhood. Maybe we can have dinner there after the movie. What do you think? Talk to you later.

Irregular Verbs

be	was/were	been	leave	left	left
become	became	become	lend	lent	lent
begin	began	begun	let	let	let
bite	bit	bitten	light	lit	lit
blow	blew	blown	lose	lost	lost
break	broke	broken	make	made	made
bring	brought	brought	mean	meant	meant
build	built	built	meet	met	met
buy	bought	bought	put	put	put
catch	caught	caught	quit	quit	quit
choose	chose	chosen	read	read	read
come	came	come	ride	rode	ridden
cost	cost	cost	ring	rang	rung
cut	cut	cut	run	ran	run
do	did	done	say	said	said
draw	drew	drawn	see	saw	seen
drink	drank	drunk	sell	sold	sold
drive	drove	driven	send	sent	sent
eat	ate	eaten	set	set	set
fall	fell	fallen	sew	sewed	sewed/sewn
feed	fed	fed	shake	shook	shaken
feel	felt	felt	shrink	shrank	shrunk
fight	fought	fought	sing	sang	sung
find	found	found	sit	sat	sat
fit	fit	fit	sleep	slept	slept
fly	flew	flown	speak	spoke	spoken
forget	forgot	forgotten	spend	spent	spent
forgive	forgave	forgiven	stand	stood	stood
freeze	froze	frozen	steal	stole	stolen
get	got	gotten	sweep	swept	swept
give	gave	given	swim	swam	swum
go	went	gone	take	took	taken
grow	grew	grown	teach	taught	taught
hang	hung	hung	tell	told	told
have	had	had	think	thought	thought
hear	heard	heard	throw	threw	thrown
hide	hid	hidden	understand	understood	understood
hit	hit	hit	wake	woke	woken
hold	held	held	wear	wore	worn
hurt	hurt	hurt	win	won	won
keep	kept	kept	wind	wound	wound
know	knew	known	write	wrote	written
lead	led	led			

Thematic Glossary

Actions and Activities

accept 119
act 4
adjust 29
afford 139
allow 142
answer 35
appreciate 78
approve 145
argue 8
arrange 145
arrive 25
ask 29
ask for a raise 67
assemble 29
attend 26
avoid 81
baby-sit 141
bake 2
bark 70
be located 103
begin 25
behave 142
believe 61
bite 91
born 33
borrow 28
box 87
break 11
bring 66
bring along 98
bring back 102
browse 26
build 24
bump into 102
buy 11
call 7
call on 124
call up 116
can 3
cancel 107
can't stand 81
catch 145
catch a cold 107
change 33
chat online 3
check 33
chew 105
choose 145
chop 14
circle 148
clean 2
clean up 123
close 35
collect 114
come 19
come from 33
come home 66
come over 125
commute 140
compete 111
complain 8
compose 2
consider 81
continue 81
cook 2
cost 127
count 57
cover 13
crash 111
cross 113
cross out 115

cry 13
cut 11
dance 4
date 69
decide 33
decline 148
deliver 12
describe 65
deserve 109
direct traffic 69
disagree 142
discuss 95
dislocate 105
do 3
do business 65
do card tricks 97
do gymnastics 105
do homework 27
do over 119
do research 26
do sit-ups 69
do the tango 105
do yoga 38
draw 38
drink 13
drive 4
drop off 122
earn 109
eat 2
eat out 96
end 100
enjoy 31
enroll 92
envy 86
erase 119
examine 145
excuse 83
exercise 3
exist 66
expect 140
explain 41
express 68
fail 106
fall 11
fall asleep 13
fall for 147
fall off 113
fall through 108
feed 46
feel 17
feel better 104
feel like 120
fight 14
figure out 123
figure skate 87
fill out 26
find 30
finish 13
fire 108
fit 127
fix 28
fly 30
fly a kite 95
follow 44
forget 13
get 15
get a promotion 109
get along 125
get around 19
get cold feet 108
get hurt 105
get off 14
get on 30

get out 25
get over 124
get ready 108
get rid of 44
get sick 107
get stuck 40
get there 18
get together 122
get up 31
give 33
give a party 97
give back 119
give blood 42
give up 111
go 6
go back 89
go bowling 42
go by 100
go camping 32
go canoeing 95
go dancing 44
go fishing 62
go kayaking 45
go out with 23
go shopping 66
go swimming 35
go to bed 46
go together 106
go window-shopping 95
go with 128
gossip 85
graduate 56
grow 113
grow up 5
growl 17
guess 88
hand in 115
hang up 115
happen 17
hate 81
have 19
have to 35
hear 35
hear from 124
help 44
hide 131
hike 14
hold 113
hook up 115
hope 35
hurt 11
ice skate 26
imagine 30
immigrate 34
include 111
injure 104
interrupt 85
interview 112
invite 108
involve 146
iron 2
jog 17
jump 17
keep 17
keep on 81
kid 74
kiss 131
knit 2
know 34
last 66
lay off 140

lead 146
leak 69
learn 81
leave 30
leave on 119
lend 28
light 146
like 4
listen 9
live 9
look 16
look for 69
look forward to 31
look through 98
look up 119
look up to 125
lose 11
major in 136
make 23
make a list 67
marry 33
may 68
mean 68
meet 11
memorize 95
mend 69
miss 30
move 30
move out 102
must 114
need 35
notice 128
offer 136
open 35
operate 65
oppose 137
order 67
own 53
pack 35
paint 2
pass 33
pass by 102
pay 26
pay attention 113
peel 69
perform 95
pick 69
pick on 124
pick out 115
pick up 66
pin 146
place 111
plan 107
plant 75
play 3
play baseball 3
play Bingo 43
play cards 23
play chess 141
play golf 82
play hide and seek 101
play Monopoly 45
play Scrabble 3
play sports 4
play squash 105
play tennis 24
poke 14
practice 3
prefer 140
prepare 14
promise 73
purchase 95
put 113
put away 115
put on 99
put to bed 66

quit 81
rain 24
read 2
realize 16
receive 67
recommend 112
refuse 129
rehearse 95
relax 31
remember 95
rent 48
repair 49
represent 111
resemble 148
respect 143
rest 44
retire 89
return 25
ride 11
ring 69
rip 14
roller-skate 104
run 71
run away 99
run into 124
run out of 124
sail away 100
say 35
say good-bye 30
say hello 102
scuba dive 40
see 17
seem 114
sell 65
send 8
serve 34
shake 17
shave 14
shine 95
shoot 113
shop 26
shout 8
shovel 98
sing 4
sit 16
skate 4
ski 4
sleep 12
slip 117
snow 71
snowboard 14
speak 11
spend 34
sprain 105
stand 16
stand in line 69
stand up 147
start 58
stay 5
stay home 35
stay open 65
stay up 99
stop 81
study 2
submit 145
support 137
surf 87
swim 3
switch 65
take 13
take a shower 66
take a trip 102
take a walk 37
take after 125
take back 116
take care 34
take down 115

take home 109
take off 100
take out 121
talk 7
tap dance 87
teach 11
tease 91
tell 5
tend to 137
thank 35
think 24
think about 81
think over 119
throw 146
throw away 115
throw out 116
train 107
travel 35
trip 14
try 44
try on 115
turn down 119
turn off 35
turn on 98
twist 104
type 4
understand 68
use 35
use up 119
vacuum 49
visit 8
wait 47
wake up 115
walk 102
walk home 128
walk the dog 131
want 5
wash 12
watch 3
watch TV 9
water 95
water-ski 24
wave 16
wear 23
weight train 111
win 109
wish 146
work 9
work late 108
work out 26
work overtime 26
worry 91
wrestle 95
write 2
write down 119

Ailments, Symptoms, and Injuries

backache 60
black and blue 54
black eye 14
break *his* leg 14
break *his* tooth 105
burn *themselves* 14
cut *himself* 14
dislocate *her* shoulder 105
feel dizzy 54
fever 54
flu 124
headache 54
heart attack 105
hurt *himself* 14
injure *her* knee 104
lose *his* voice 105
measles 53

153

Index

ACTIVITY WORKBOOK

SIDE by SIDE

THIRD EDITION

BOOK 3

Steven J. Molinsky
Bill Bliss

with

Carolyn Graham

Contributing Authors

Dorothy Lynde • Elizabeth Handley

Illustrated by
Richard E. Hill

Side by Side, 3rd edition
Activity Workbook 3

Pearson Education, 10 Bank Street, White Plains, NY 10606

Vice president, director of publishing: *Allen Ascher*
Editorial manager: *Pam Fishman*
Vice president, director of design and production: *Rhea Banker*
Associate director of electronic production: *Aliza Greenblatt*
Production manager: *Ray Keating*
Director of manufacturing: *Patrice Fraccio*
Associate digital layout manager: *Paula D. Williams*
Editorial supervisor: *Janet Johnston*
Digital layout specialist: *Lisa Ghiozzi*
Interior design: *Wendy Wolf*
Cover design: *Elizabeth Carlson*

Illustrator: *Richard E. Hill*

The authors gratefully acknowledge the contribution
of Tina Carver in the development of the original
Side by Side program.

Longman on the Web
Longman.com offers classroom activities, teaching tips and online resources for teachers of all levels and students of all ages. Visit us for course-specific Companion Websites, our comprehensive online catalog of all Longman titles, and access to all local Longman websites, offices and contacts around the world.

Join a global community of teachers and students at **Longman.com**.

Longman English Success offers online courses to give learners flexible, self-paced study options. Developed for distance learning or to complement classroom instruction, courses cover General English, Business English, and Exam Preparation.

For more information visit **EnglishSuccess.com**.

ISBN 0-13-026875-5

Printed in the United States of America

14 15 – CRK – 09 08 07

CONTENTS

what	bake	cook	move	sit
where	compose	go	read	watch

1. A. _____What's_____ Fran _____reading_____?

   B. _____She's reading_____ her e-mail.

2. A. _____Where's_____ Fred _____?

   B. _____ to the clinic.

3. A. _____ Nancy _____?

   B. _____ a game show.

4. A. _____ you _____?

   B. _____ dinner.

5. A. _____ you and your wife

      _____?

   B. _____ to Miami.

6. A. _____ your grandmother

   and grandfather _____?

   B. _____ in the park.

7. A. _____ Victor _____?

   B. _____ a symphony.

8. A. _____ you _____?

   B. _____ an apple pie.

B ON THE PHONE

1.
A. Hi. What ____are____ you doing?

B. ___I'm watching___ a movie on TV.

A. Oh. I don't want to disturb you. _____ Anna busy?

B. Yes, _____. _____ a bath.

A. I'll call back later.

2.
A. Hi, Bill. _____ the children okay?

B. Yes. _____ fine.

A. What _____ doing?

B. Vicky _____ her homework, and

Timmy _____ baseball in the yard.

A. How about you? _____ doing?

B. _____ dinner for you and the kids.

A. I'll be home soon.

3.
A. Hello, Peter. This is Mr. Taylor. _____ your father at home?

B. No, _____. _____ at the health club.

A. Can I speak to your mother?

B. I'm sorry. _____ busy right now. _____ the washing machine. It's broken.

A. Okay. I'll call back later.

4.
A. Hello, _____. Can I speak to _____?

B. I'm sorry. _____.

A. Well, can I speak to _____?

B. I'm afraid _____.

A. Okay. I'll call back later.

Activity Workbook   **3**

C YOU DECIDE: *Why Is Today Different?*

1. *(clean)* I never _____clean_____ my apartment, but _____I'm cleaning_____ it today

   because _____my grandmother is going to visit me (or) my boss is coming over for dinner_____ .

2. *(iron)* Roger never _____ his shirts, but _____ them today

   because _____ .

3. *(argue)* We never _____ with our landlord, but _____ with him today

   because _____ .

4. *(worry)* I never _____ about anything, but _____ today because

   _____ .

5. *(watch)* Betty never _____ the news, but _____ it today because

   _____ .

6. *(write)* Uncle Phil never _____ to us, but _____ to us today

   because _____ .

7. *(take)* I never _____ the bus, but _____ it today because

   _____ .

8. *(comb)* My son never _____ his hair, but _____ it today

   because _____ .

9. *(get up)* My daughter never _____ early, but _____ early today

   because _____ .

10. *(smile)* Mr. Grimes never _____ , but _____ today because

    _____ .

11. *(bark)* Our dogs never _____ , but _____ today

    because _____ .

12. *(wear)* Alice never _____ perfume, but _____ it today

    because _____ .

WHAT ARE THEY SAYING?

1. I recommend the fish.   <u>Do you recommend</u> the chicken, too?

2. My husband bakes delicious cakes.   _____ he _____ pies, too?

3. My daughter gets up early.   _____ your son _____ early, too?

4. They always complain about the traffic.   _____ they _____ about the weather, too?

5. Maria speaks Italian and Spanish.   _____ she _____ French, too?

6. My grandson lives in Miami.   _____ your granddaughter _____ there, too?

7. I watch the news every morning.   _____ every evening, too?

8. My sister plays soccer.   _____ tennis, too?

9. Robert practices the trombone at night.   _____ during the day, too?

10. We plant vegetables every year.   _____ flowers, too?

11. Stanley always adds salt to the stew.   _____ pepper, too?

12. I always wear a jacket to work.   _____ a tie, too?

13. My cousin Sue rides a motorcycle.   _____ a bicycle, too?

14. My grandfather jogs every day.   _____ when it rains?

15. We need bread from the supermarket.   _____ milk, too?

16. Gregory always irons his shirts.   _____ his pants, too?

17. Our neighbors have three dogs.   _____ any cats?

E PUZZLE

Across

3. I like to cook. I'm an excellent _____ .
4. I can type. I'm a very good _____ .
5. Sally swims fast. She's a fast _____ .
6. Jeff likes to play sports. He's a good
   _____ .
7. My sons drive taxis. They're both taxi
   _____ .

Down

1. You ski well. You're a very good _____ .
2. We act in plays and movies. We're _____ .
5. My children love to skate They're
   wonderful _____ .

F WHAT'S THE ANSWER?

Circle the correct answer.

1. Does Hector like to play tennis?
   a. Yes, he likes.
   b. Yes, he does.
   c. Yes, he is.

2. Are you a graceful dancer?
   a. No, I don't.
   b. No, you aren't.
   c. No, I'm not.

3. Does your boss work hard?
   a. Yes, he is.
   b. Yes, he does.
   c. Yes, he works.

4. Is the food at this restaurant spicy?
   a. Yes, it isn't.
   b. Yes, it does.
   c. Yes, it is.

5. Are your children good athletes?
   a. Yes, I am.
   b. Yes, they are.
   c. Yes, they do.

6. Do you and your girlfriend like to cook?
   a. Yes, she does.
   b. Yes, they do.
   c. Yes, we do.

7. Am I a good teacher?
   a. Yes, you are.
   b. Yes, he is.
   c. Yes, you do.

8. Does your husband send e-mail messages to you?
   a. Yes, he is.
   b. Yes, he does.
   c. Yes, she does.

WHAT ARE THEY SAYING?

1. A. I _____don't_____ like to eat at Albert's house because he _____ cook very well.

   B. I know. Everybody says he _____ a very good _____ .

2. A. I know you _____ like to drive with me because you think _____ a terrible driver.

   B. That's not true. I think you _____ very carefully!

3. A. _____ like to type?

   B. No, I _____ . _____ not a very accurate typist.

   A. I disagree. _____ an accurate typist, but you _____ very slowly.

4. A. Oliver Jones is an excellent composer.

   B. I agree. He _____ beautifully. I think _____ very talented.

5. A. Irene _____ going swimming with us today because she _____ like to swim when it's cold.

   B. That's too bad. I really like to go swimming with her. She's a very good _____ .

6. A. I'm jealous of my classmates. They speak English very well, and I _____ .

   B. That's not true. Your classmates _____ English clearly, but you're a good English _____ , too.

H **LISTENING** 🔊

Listen to each question and then complete the answer.

1. Yes, _____he does_____ .

2. No, _____she isn't_____ .

3. Yes, _____ .

4. Yes, _____ .

5. No, _____ .

6. Yes, _____ .

7. No, _____ .

8. Yes, _____ .

9. No, _____ .

10. Yes, _____ .

11. No, _____ .

12. Yes, _____ .

13. Yes, _____ .

14. No, _____ .

15. No, _____ .

Listen. Then clap and practice.

A.   Does he like   the movies?

B.   No,   he doesn't.   He likes   TV.

A. Does she like   the mountains?

B.   No,   she doesn't.   She likes   the sea.

A.   Do you like to   hike?

B.   No,   I don't.   I like to   dive.

A. Do they like to   walk?

B.   No,   they don't.   They like to   drive.

A.   Is he studying   music?

B.   No,   he isn't.   He's studying   math.

A.   Is she taking   a shower?

B.   No,   she isn't.   She's taking   a bath.

A. Are they living   in Brooklyn?

B.   No,   they aren't. They're living   in Queens.

A. Are you washing   your shirt?

B.   No,   I'm not.   I'm washing   my jeans.

J WHAT'S THE QUESTION?

1. We're waiting for <u>the bus</u>.   What are you waiting for?

2. He's thinking about <u>his girlfriend</u>.   Who is he thinking about?

3. They're ironing <u>their shirts</u>. _____

4. I'm calling <u>my landlord</u>. _____

5. She's dancing with <u>her father</u>. _____

6. He's watching <u>the news</u>. _____

7. They're complaining about <u>the rent</u>. _____

8. She's playing baseball with <u>her son</u>. _____

9. They're visiting <u>their cousins</u>. _____

10. We're looking at <u>the animals in the zoo</u>. _____

11. I'm writing about <u>my favorite movie</u>. _____

12. He's arguing with <u>his boss</u>. _____

13. She's knitting a sweater for <u>her daughter</u>. _____

14. We're making <u>pancakes</u>. _____

15. I'm sending an e-mail to <u>my uncle</u>. _____

16. They're worrying about <u>their examination</u>. _____

17. She's talking to <u>the soccer coach</u>. _____

18. He's skating with <u>his grandparents</u>. _____

K WHAT ARE THEY SAYING?

1. A. Where are you and your husband taking ____your____ children?

   B. __We're__ taking ____them____ to the zoo.

2. A. Why is Richard calling all _____ friends today?

   B. _____ wants to tell _____ about _____ new car.

3. A. What are your parents going to give you for your birthday?

   B. I'm not sure, but _____ might give _____ a puppy.

4. A. Why is Susie visiting _____ grandparents?

   B. _____ wants to show _____ her new bicycle.

5. A. Why are you wearing a safety helmet on _____ head?

   B. _____ don't want to hurt _____ head while I'm skateboarding.

6. A. Where are you taking _____ new girlfriend on Saturday night?

   B. _____ taking _____ to see the new science fiction movie downtown.

7. A. Why are those students complaining about their teacher?

   B. _____ think she gives _____ too much homework.

8. A. Can I tell you and Dad about the party now?

   B. No. We're sleeping now. You can tell _____ about _____ tomorrow morning.

9. A. Why is Mrs. Jenkins waiting for the plumber?

   B. The sink is leaking. Charlie, the plumber, says _____ can fix _____.

10. A. Timmy, why are you arguing with _____ sister?

    B. _____ wants to play with _____ new toys, but she can't. They're mine.

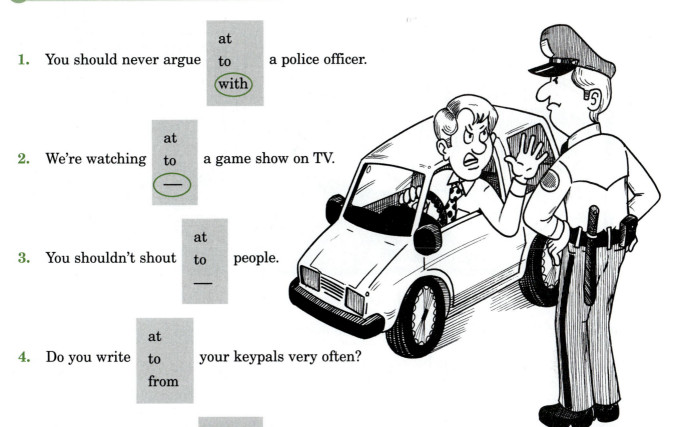

1. You should never argue [at / to / (with)] a police officer.

2. We're watching [at / to / (—)] a game show on TV.

3. You shouldn't shout [at / to / —] people.

4. Do you write [at / to / from] your keypals very often?

5. They always complain [at / — / about] the weather.

6. We visit [at / to / —] our sister's friends in Texas once a year.

7. I'm helping [at / to / —] my neighbors [to / with / —] their garden.

8. I'm always frustrated when I have to wait [for / at] the bus.

9. Call [to / at] the exterminator right away!

2

Herbert *(have)* ___had___ [1] a very bad day yesterday. He usually gets up early, but yesterday morning he *(get up)* _____ [2] very late! He *(eat)* _____ [3] breakfast quickly, *(rush)* _____ [4] out of the house, and *(run)* _____ [5] to the bus stop. Unfortunately, he *(miss)* _____ [6] the bus. He *(wait)* _____ [7] for ten minutes, but there weren't any more buses, so he *(decide)* _____ [8] to walk to his office. Herbert was upset. He *(arrive)* _____ [9] at work two and a half hours late!

Herbert *(sit)* _____ [10] down at his desk and *(begin)* _____ [11] his work. He *(call)* _____ [12] a few people on the telephone, and he *(type)* _____ [13] a few letters. But he was in a hurry, and he *(make)* _____ [14] a lot of mistakes. He *(fix)* _____ [15] the mistakes, but when he *(finish)* _____ [16] the letters and *(put)* _____ [17] them on his desk, he *(spill)* _____ [18] water all over them.

At noon, Herbert *(go)* _____ [19] to the company cafeteria and *(order)* _____ [20] a pizza for lunch. That was a big mistake. The pizza was very spicy, and Herbert *(feel)* _____ [21] sick for the rest of the day.

Herbert's afternoon was even worse than his morning. He *(forget)* _____ [22] about an important meeting, his computer *(crash)* _____ [23], he *(fall)* _____ [24] asleep at his desk, his chair *(break)* _____ [25], and he *(hurt)* _____ [26] his arm.

Herbert *(leave)* _____ [27] the office at 5:00, *(take)* _____ [28] the bus home, and immediately *(go)* _____ [29] to bed! What a terrible, terrible day!

Listen and circle the correct answer.

1. yesterday
   (every day)

2. **(yesterday)**
   every day

3. yesterday
   every day

4. yesterday
   every day

5. yesterday
   every day

6. yesterday
   every day

7. yesterday
   every day

8. yesterday
   every day

9. yesterday
   every day

10. yesterday
    every day

11. yesterday
    every day

12. yesterday
    every day

C WHAT'S THE WORD?

Fill in the missing words. Then read the story aloud.

| decide | lift | need | paint | plant | roller-blade | wait | want |

Last Saturday everyone ___wanted___ ¹ my help. In the morning, I

_____ ² heavy furniture for my wife, and I _____ ³ the

bathroom walls. Then I _____ ⁴ in the park with my son and

_____ ⁵ flowers with my daughter. In the afternoon, my brother

_____ ⁶ my help. I went to a store with him and _____ ⁷

while he _____ ⁸ which suit to buy for his wedding.

D PUZZLE: *What Did They Do?*

Across
2. ride
3. teach
5. are
6. meet
7. deliver

Down
1. write
4. get
5. work

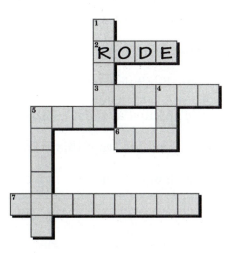

WHAT'S THE QUESTION?

1. _____*Did you buy*_____ the green one?   No, I didn't. I bought the blue one.

2. _____ a plane?   No, they didn't. They took a boat.

3. _____ a movie?   No, she didn't. She saw a play.

4. _____ French?   No, he didn't. He spoke Arabic.

5. _____ your arm?   No, I didn't. I broke my leg.

6. _____ at seven?   No, it didn't. It began at eight.

7. _____ to Paris?   No, she didn't. She flew to Rome.

8. _____ the beef?   No, we didn't. We had the chicken.

9. _____ with you?   No, they didn't. They went alone.

10. _____ too softly?   No, you didn't. You sang too loudly.

11. _____ your mother?   No, he didn't. He met my father.

12. _____ your keys?   No, I didn't. I lost my ring.

F **WHAT'S THE ANSWER?**

| was | were |
| wasn't | weren't |

| angry | hungry | prepared | scared | tired |
| bored | on time | sad | thirsty | |

1. The students fell asleep in Professor Winter's class because _____*they were bored*_____.

2. I didn't finish my sandwich today because _____*I wasn't hungry*_____.

3. They went to bed early last night because _____.

4. She didn't do well on the test because _____.

5. He shouted at them because _____.

6. I missed the train this morning because _____.

7. My daughter didn't finish all her milk because _____.

8. I covered my eyes during the movie because _____.

9. They cried when they said good-bye at the airport because _____.

1. Albert usually drives very carefully.

   He _____*didn't drive*_____ carefully yesterday afternoon.

   He _____*drove*_____ much too fast.

2. Alice usually comes home from work early.

   She _____ home early last night.

   She _____ home late.

3. I usually take the bus to work.

   I _____ the bus this morning.

   I _____ the train.

4. We usually go to the movies on Saturday.

   We _____ to the movies last Saturday.

   We _____ to a concert.

5. Carl and Tom usually forget their homework.

   They _____ their homework yesterday.

   They _____ their lunch.

6. Mr. Tyler usually wears a suit to the office.

   He _____ a suit today.

   He _____ jeans.

7. Professor Hall usually teaches biology.

   She _____ biology last semester.

   She _____ astronomy.

8. Mr. and Mrs. Miller usually eat dinner at 7:00.

   They _____ dinner at 7:00 last night.

   They _____ at 9:00.

9. My grandmother usually gives me a tie for my birthday.

   She _____ me a tie this year.

   She _____ me a watch.

10. Alan usually sits by himself in English class.

    He _____ by himself today.

    He _____ with all his friends.

11. I usually have cereal for breakfast.

    I _____ cereal this morning.

    I _____ eggs.

12. Amanda usually sings very beautifully.

    She _____ beautifully last night.

    She _____ very badly.

1. A. _____Did you_____ clean your apartment this week?

   B. No, I _____didn't_____ . I _____was_____ too lazy.

2. A. _____ meet the company president at the office party?

   B. No, we _____. But we _____ his wife.

3. A. _____ Richard fall?

   B. Yes, he _____. He skated very quickly, and he _____ very careful.

4. A. _____ Rita deliver all the pizzas today?

   B. No, _____. The people at 10 Main Street _____ home.

5. A. _____ Roger _____ asleep at the meeting this morning?

   B. No, _____. But he _____ asleep later in his office. He _____ very tired.

6. A. _____ you ride your motorcycle to work today?

   B. No, _____. I _____ my bicycle, and I _____ late. My supervisor _____ upset.

7. A. _____ like the movie?

   B. Yes, I _____. It _____ great!
   How about you? Did you like it?

   A. No, I _____. I thought it

   _____ boring.

9. A. _____ you complain to your
   landlord about the problems in your
   apartment?

   B. Yes, we _____. He listened to

   us, but he _____ fix anything.

   We _____ very angry.

11. A. Dad, _____ you buy anything at
    the supermarket?

    B. Yes, _____. I _____
    some food for dinner.

    A. _____ buy any ice cream?

    B. Sorry. I _____. There

    _____ any.

8. A. _____ Mrs. Sanchez your
   Spanish teacher last semester?

   B. Yes, she _____. _____ you
   in her class?

   A. No, _____. I _____
   take Spanish. I took French.

10. A. _____ the students dance
    gracefully in the school play?

    B. No, _____. They

    _____ very awkwardly. They

    _____ very nervous.

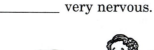

12. A. Grandpa, _____ you a good

    soccer player when you _____
    young?

    B. Yes, _____. I _____

    a very good player. I _____ fast,

    and I _____ clumsy.

1. How did Steven sprain his ankle? *(play tennis)*

   <u>He sprained his ankle while he was playing tennis.</u>

2. How did your sister rip her pants? *(exercise)*

   _____

3. How did you break your arm? *(play volleyball)*

   _____

4. How did James poke himself in the eye? *(fix his sink)*

   _____

5. How did you and your brother hurt yourselves? *(skateboard)*

   _____

6. How did Mr. and Mrs. Davis trip and fall? *(dance)*

   _____

7. How did your father burn himself? *(cook french fries)*

   _____

8. How did your daughter get a black eye? *(fight with the kid across the street)*

   _____

9. How did you cut yourself? *(chop carrots)*

   _____

10. How did Robert lose his cell phone? *(jog in the park)*

    _____

11. How did you _____?

    _____

J **GRAMMARRAP:** *What Did He Do?*

Listen. Then clap and practice.

A.   What did he   do?

B.   He did   his homework.

A.   What did she   sing?

B.   She sang   a song.

A.   What did they   hide?

B.   They hid   their money.

A.   Where did you   go?

B.   I went to   Hong Kong.

A.   What did he   lose?

B.   He lost his   watch.

A.   What did he   study?

B.   He studied   French.

A.   What did it   cost?

B.   It cost   a lot.

A.   What did they   buy?

B.   They bought   a wrench.

K **GRAMMARRAP:** *I Was Talking to Bob When I Ran Into Sue*

Listen. Then clap and practice.

I was talking to   Bob when   I ran into   Sue.

I was waiting for   Jack when   I saw   Mary Lou.

They were cleaning   the house when   I knocked on the door.

He was dusting   a lamp when   it fell   on the floor.

She was learning to   drive when   I met her   last May.

She was buying   a car when   I saw her   today.

How	What	Where
How long	What kind of	Who
How many	When	Why

1. _____Who did you meet?_____   I met <u>the president</u>.

2. _____   She lost <u>her purse</u>.

3. _____   We did our exercises <u>at the beach</u>.

4. _____   They left <u>at 9:15</u>.

5. _____   She got here <u>by plane</u>.

6. _____   He sang <u>in a concert hall</u>.

7. _____   They stayed <u>for a week</u>.

8. _____   I saw a <u>science fiction</u> movie.

9. _____   He cried <u>because the movie was sad</u>.

10. _____   She wrote a letter to <u>her brother</u>.

11. _____   They complained about <u>the telephone bill</u>.

12. _____   We ate <u>a lot of</u> grapes.

13. _____   He spoke <u>at the meeting</u>.

14. _____   They lifted weights <u>all morning</u>.

15. _____   She gave a present to <u>her cousin</u>.

16. _____   I ordered <u>apple</u> pie.

17. _____   We rented <u>seven</u> videos.

18. _____   They sent an e-mail to <u>their teacher</u>.

19. _____   He fell asleep <u>during the lecture</u>.

20. _____   I lost my hat <u>while I was skiing</u>.

1. A. Did you go to Hong Kong?

    B. No, _____we didn't_____ .

    A. Where _____did you go_____ ?

    B. _____We went_____ to Tokyo.

3. A. Did your flight to Japan leave on time?

    B. No, _____ .

    A. How late _____

        _____ ?

    B. _____ two hours late.

5. A. Did you stay in a big hotel?

    B. No, _____ .

    A. What kind of _____

        _____ ?

    B. _____ .

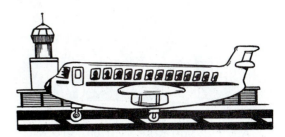

2. A. Did you get there by boat?

    B. No, _____ .

    A. How _____ ?

    B. _____ .

4. A. Did you have good weather during the flight?

    B. No, _____ .

    A. What kind of _____

        _____ ?

    B. _____ terrible weather.

6. A. Did you eat American food?

    B. No, _____ .

    A. What kind of _____

        _____ ?

    B. _____ .

(continued)

7. A. Did you take your camera with you?

B. No, _____.

A. What _____

_____?

B. _____ our camcorder.

9. A. Did you meet many Japanese?

B. No, _____.

A. Who _____?

B. _____ other tourists.

Where's the train station?

11. A. Did you speak Japanese?

B. No, _____.

A. What language _____

_____?

B. _____.

8. A. Did you get around the city by train?

B. No, _____.

A. How _____

_____?

B. _____.

10. A. Did you buy any clothing?

B. No, _____.

A. What _____?

B. _____ souvenirs.

12. A. Did you spend a lot of money?

B. Yes, _____.

A. How much _____

_____?

B. _____.

N SOUND IT OUT!

Listen to each word and then say it.

th**i**s			th**e**se		

this

1. ch**i**cken   3. r**i**ver   5. b**u**sy
2. m**i**ddle   4. k**i**d   6. d**i**dn't

these

1. ch**ee**se   3. asl**ee**p   5. St**e**ve
2. m**ea**t   4. rec**ei**ve   6. rep**ea**t

Listen and put a circle around the word that has the same sound.

1. cl**ea**n: f**i**ne   m**i**ddle   **(these)**
2. m**i**x: sk**i**   d**i**d   n**ee**d
3. **ea**sy: R**i**ta   br**ea**k   **e**yes
4. v**i**deo: mach**i**ne   b**i**g   k**ee**p
5. **ea**st: bu**i**ld   l**i**ttle   gr**ee**n
6. s**y**mphony: m**i**ttens   l**i**fe   ret**i**re
7. r**i**p: kn**ee**   mayb**e**   kn**i**t

Now make a sentence using all the words you circled, and read the sentence aloud.

8. ....
....

9. m**ea**t: Gr**ee**k   **I**nternet   **ei**ght
10. sp**i**ll: h**ea**lthy   h**i**s   rain**y**
11. prom**i**se: ch**i**ld   k**e**y   R**i**chard
12. t**ea**:   ever**y**   m**e**n   **i**nto
13. cook**ie**:   w**i**th   sp**ea**ks   br**i**cks
14. m**i**lk: m**i**ne   adv**i**ce   w**i**th
15. t**ea**m: **i**s   w**ee**k   attract**i**ve
16. t**y**pical: s**i**ster   laz**y**   r**e**build

Now make a sentence using all the words you circled, and read the sentence aloud.

17. ....
....

A WHAT ARE THEY SAYING?

1. A. Did you ride your bicycle to work this morning?

    B. <u>No, I didn't</u>. I <u>rode</u> my

    motorcycle. <u>I'm going to ride</u> my bicycle to work tomorrow morning.

2. A. Did Tommy wear his new shoes to school today?

    B. _____. He _____

    his old shoes. _____ his new shoes tomorrow.

3. A. Did Sally give her husband a sweater for his birthday this year?

    B. _____. She _____

    him a tie. _____
    him a sweater next year.

4. A. Did your parents drive to the mountains last weekend?

    B. _____. They _____ to

    the beach. _____
    to the mountains next weekend.

5. A. Did you and your family have eggs for breakfast this morning?

    B. _____. We _____

    pancakes. _____
    eggs tomorrow morning.

6. A. Did you go out with Mandy last Saturday night?

    B. _____. I _____

    out with Sandy. _____
    out with Mandy next Saturday night.

7. A. Did Howard write an interesting story for homework today?

    B. _____. He _____ a

    boring one. _____
    a more interesting story next time.

8. A. Did Shirley leave the office early this afternoon?

    B. _____. She _____

    very late. _____
    early tomorrow afternoon.

1. I'm really scared. Tomorrow my dentist is going to ##########.

I'm sorry. I can't hear you. I think we have a bad connection. What's _your dentist going to do_?

2. We're very excited about our trip. We're going to go to ##########.

What did you say? I can't hear you. Where _____ _____?

3. My son is very sad. His girlfriend is going to move to Alaska because #############.

I'm sorry. We have a bad connection. Why _____ _____?

4. My parents are going to give me a ########## for my sixteenth birthday.

Excuse me. I can't hear you. _____ _____?

5. I'm really nervous. I'm going to ########## for the first time tomorrow.

We have a bad connection. _____ _____?

6. Please come to our wedding. We're going to get married next ##########.

I'm sorry. I can't hear you. _____ _____?

7. I won't be home after school today. I'm going to meet ##########.

This is a terrible connection! _____ _____?

(continued)

Listen and choose the time of the action.

1. a. last night
   (b.) tomorrow night

2. a. yesterday afternoon
   b. tomorrow afternoon

3. a. this weekend
   b. last weekend

4. a. this Saturday
   b. last Saturday

5. a. last week
   b. next week

6. a. yesterday evening
   b. this evening

7. a. tomorrow night
   b. last night

8. a. this weekend
   b. last weekend

9. a. this evening
   b. yesterday evening

10. a. last winter
    b. this winter

11. a. tomorrow morning
    b. yesterday morning

12. a. next semester
    b. last semester

James is a pessimist. He always thinks the worst will happen.

All his friends are optimists. They always tell James he shouldn't worry.

1. I'm afraid I ____won't have____ a good time at the office party tomorrow.

   Yes, ____you will____. ____You'll____ have a wonderful time.

2. I'm sure my son ____will hurt____ himself in his soccer match today.

   No, ____he won't____. ____He won't____ hurt himself. He's always very careful.

3. I'm afraid my grandmother _____ get out of the hospital soon.

   Yes, _____. _____ get out of the hospital in a few days.

4. I'm afraid my wife _____ upset if I get a very short haircut.

   No, _____. _____ be upset.

5. I'm positive I _____ weight on my new diet.

   Yes, _____. _____ lose a lot of weight.

6. I'm afraid my children _____ my birthday this year.

   No, _____. _____ forget your birthday. They never forget it.

7. I'm afraid my landlord _____ our broken doorbell.

   Yes, _____. _____ fix it as soon as he can.

8. I'm afraid my new neighbors _____ like me.

   Of course _____. _____ you a lot. Everybody likes you.

9. I'm sure _____ catch a cold when we go camping this weekend.

   No, _____. _____ catch a cold, James. You worry too much!

E **WHAT WILL BE HAPPENING?**

attend	browse	clean	do	fill out	rain	watch	work out

1. A. Will Amanda be busy this afternoon?

   B. Yes, ___she will___.

   ___She'll be doing___ research at the library.

2. A. Will you be busy this evening?

   B. Yes, _____. _____

   _____ my income tax form.

3. A. Will Donald be home this afternoon?

   B. No, _____. _____

   _____ at his health club.

4. A. Will Mr. and Mrs. Lee be busy tonight?

   B. Yes, _____. _____

   _____ their apartment.

5. A. Will Grandpa be busy tonight?

   B. Yes, _____. _____

   _____ the web until after midnight.

6. A. Will you and your wife be home today?

   B. Yes, _____. _____

   _____ our favorite game show on TV.

7. A. Will Mom be home early tonight?

   B. No, _____. _____

   _____ a meeting.

8. A. Will the weather be nice this weekend?

   B. No, _____. _____

   _____ cats and dogs!

A TOUR OF MY CITY

Pretend you're taking people on a tour of your city or town. Fill in the blanks with real places you know.

> Good morning, everybody. This is .... speaking. I'm
> so glad you'll be coming with me today on a tour of ....
> We'll be leaving in just a few minutes.
>
> First, I'll be taking you to see my favorite places in the city: ....,
> ...., and ....
> Then we'll be going to .... for lunch. In my opinion, this is
> the best restaurant in town. After that, I'll be taking you to see the other interesting
> tourist sights: ...., ...,
> and .... This evening we'll be going to ....
> .... I'm sure you'll have a wonderful time.

G **WHAT ARE THEY SAYING?**

1. A. I'm sorry. I can't talk right now. I'm

   _____giving_____ the kids a bath.

   B. How much longer _will you be giving_
      them a bath?

2. A. How much longer _____

      _____ your homework?

   B. I'll probably _____
      my homework for another half hour.

   A. Okay. I'll call you then.

3. A. Hi, Carol. This is Bob. Can you

      _____ for a minute?

   B. Sorry. I can't _____ right now.

      I'm _____ for a big test.

4. A. Sorry, Alan. I can't talk now. I'm

      _____ dinner with my family.

   B. How much longer _____

      _____ dinner?

Listen. Then clap and practice.

A. Will you   be home   at a quarter   to three?
B. Yes,   I will.   I'll be watching   TV.

A. Will John   be home   at half   past two?
B. Yes,   he will.   He'll be cooking   some stew.

A. Will your parents   be home   today   at four?
B. Yes,   they will.   They'll be washing   the floor.

A. Will Jane   be home   if I call   at one?
B. Yes,   she will.   She'll be feeding   her son.

A. Will you   be home   at half   past eight?
B. No,   I won't.   I'll be working   late.

A. Will John   be home   at a quarter   to ten?
B. No,   he won't.   He'll be visiting   a friend.

A. Will your parents   be home   tonight   at nine?
B. No,   they won't.   They'll be standing   in line.

A. Will Jane   be home   if I call her   at seven?
B. No,   she won't.   She'll be dancing   with Kevin.

I WHOSE IS IT?

mine	his	hers	ours	yours	theirs

A. Hi, Robert. I found this wallet in my office today. Is it _____yours_____[1]?

B. No, it isn't _____[2], but it might be Tom's.

A. Maybe, but Tom hardly ever visits my office. It probably isn't _____[3].

B. It's small and blue. Maybe it's Martha's.

A. I asked her this morning. She says it isn't _____[4].

B. Is there anything inside the wallet?

A. There isn't any money, but there's a picture of three children.

B. It might belong to Mr. Hill. He and his wife have three children.

Maybe the children are _____[5].

A. I showed the picture to Mr. and Mrs. Hill. They said, "These

children aren't _____[6]. Our children are older."

B. Maybe you should give the wallet to our supervisor.

A. You know, it might be _____[7]. She has three children!

B. You're right. I'm positive it's _____[8]. I saw her children in her office last week.

J GRAMMARRAP: *Where's My Coat?*

Listen. Then clap and practice.

A. Where's   my coat?   I can't find   mine.

Is this one   mine   or yours?

B. That one is   mine.   It isn't   yours.

Yours   is next to those doors.

A. Where's our umbrella?   We can't find   ours.

Is this one   ours   or theirs?

B. That one is   theirs.   It isn't   yours.

Yours   is under those chairs.

K WHAT DOES IT MEAN?

Circle the correct answer.

1. Jim is wearing a tuxedo today.
   a. He's going to visit his grandmother.
   (b.) He's going to a wedding.
   c. He's going to work in a factory.

2. My brother has a black eye.
   a. He painted his eye.
   b. He's wearing dark glasses.
   c. He hurt his eye.

3. The teacher wasn't on time.
   a. She was early.
   b. She was late.
   c. She didn't have a good time.

4. They chatted online yesterday.
   a. They used a cell phone.
   b. They used a computer.
   c. They used a fax machine.

5. Everyone in my family is going to relax this weekend.
   a. We're going to rest this weekend.
   b. We're going to retire this weekend.
   c. We're going to return this weekend.

6. He wasn't prepared for his exam.
   a. He didn't study for the exam.
   b. He didn't take the exam.
   c. He was ready for the exam.

7. Could I ask you a favor?
   a. I want to help you.
   b. I want to give you something.
   c. I need your help.

8. It's a very emotional day for Janet.
   a. She's going to work.
   b. She's getting married.
   c. She's studying.

9. He's composing a symphony.
   a. He's writing a symphony.
   b. He's listening to a symphony.
   c. He's going to a concert.

10. George ripped his shirt.
    a. He has to wash his shirt.
    b. He has to iron his shirt.
    c. He has to sew his shirt.

11. Can I borrow your bicycle?
    a. I need your bicycle for a little while.
    b. I want to give you my bicycle.
    c. I want to buy your bicycle.

12. Every day I practice ballet.
    a. I sing every day.
    b. I play violin every day.
    c. I dance every day.

13. I'm going to lend my car to Bob today.
    a. Bob is going to drive my car.
    b. I'm going to drive Bob's car.
    c. Bob is going to give me his car.

14. Mr. and Mrs. Hansen love to talk about their grandchildren.
    a. They listen to them.
    b. They're very proud of them.
    c. They argue with them.

15. Rita did very well on her exam.
    a. She's happy.
    b. She's anxious.
    c. She's sad.

16. I'm going to repair my washing machine.
    a. I'm going to paint it.
    b. I'm going to fix it.
    c. I'm going to do laundry.

17. I need to assemble my new VCR.
    a. Can I borrow your screwdriver?
    b. Can I borrow your ladder?
    c. Can I borrow your TV?

18. I sprained my ankle.
    a. I broke my ankle.
    b. I hurt my ankle.
    c. I poked my ankle.

19. I'm going to fill out my income tax form.
- a. I'm going to return it.
- b. I'm going to read it.
- c. I'm going to answer the questions on the form.

20. They're playing Scrabble.
- a. They're playing a game.
- b. They're playing a sport.
- c. They're playing an instrument.

21. Mr. Smith is complaining to his boss.
- a. He's talking about his boss, and he's upset.
- b. He's talking to his boss, and he's happy.
- c. He's talking to his boss, and he's upset.

22. I'm going to call my wife right away.
- a. I'm going to call her immediately.
- b. I'm going to call her in a few hours.
- c. I'm going to call her when I have time.

23. My sister is an excellent athlete.
- a. She's an active person.
- b. She plays sports very well.
- c. She likes to watch sports.

24. My mother is looking forward to her retirement.
- a. She's happy about her new job.
- b. She wants to buy new tires for her car.
- c. Soon she won't have to go to work every day.

L **LISTENING:** *Looking Forward*

Listen to each story. Then answer the questions.

What Are Mr. and Mrs. Miller Looking Forward to?

1. Mr. and Mrs. Miller _____ last week.
- (a.) moved
- b. relaxed
- c. flew to Los Angeles

2. Mr. and Mrs. Miller aren't going to _____ this weekend.
- a. repaint their living room
- b. assemble their VCR
- c. relax in their yard

3. They're going to _____ next weekend.
- a. assemble their computer
- b. relax
- c. paint flowers

What's Jonathan Looking Forward to?

4. Jonathan isn't _____ today.
- a. sitting in his office
- b. thinking about his work
- c. thinking about next weekend

5. Next weekend he'll be _____.
- a. working
- b. cooking and cleaning
- c. getting married

6. On their trip to Hawaii, Jonathan and his wife won't be _____.
- a. swimming in the ocean
- b. paying bills
- c. eating in restaurants

What's Mrs. Grant Looking Forward to?

7. When she retires, Mrs. Grant will be _____.
- a. getting up early
- b. getting up late
- c. taking the bus to work

8. Mrs. Grant will _____ with her friends.
- a. go to museums
- b. work in her garden
- c. read books

9. She'll take her grandchildren to _____.
- a. the park and the beach
- b. the zoo and the beach
- c. the park and the zoo

A. Fill in the blanks.

Ex. Ann ____is____ a good skater, and

her children __skate__ well, too.

1. A. Mr. and Mrs. Lee _____
        wonderful dancers.

    B. I agree with you. They

        _____ very well.

2. A. Roger _____ very
        carelessly.

    B. I know. He's a terrible driver.

3. A. We don't swim very well.

    B. I disagree. I think _____

        excellent _____.

4. A. I type very well. I think _____

        a very good _____.

5. A. We _____ good _____,
        but we like to ski anyway.

B. Fill in the blanks.

1. A. Did you speak to Mrs. Baxter
        yesterday?

    B. No, I _____. I _____

        too busy. But I _____ to Mrs.
        Parker.

2. A. Did you buy juice when you were at
        the store?

    B. No, I _____. I forgot. But

        I _____ milk.

3. A. _____ they get up early this
        morning?

    B. No, they _____. They _____
        up very late.

4. A. Did Mr. Wong teach biology last
        semester?

    B. No, he _____. He _____
        astronomy because the astronomy

        teacher _____ sick all semester.

5. A. _____ you talk to Tom last night?

    B. No, I _____. I _____ to

        his wife. Tom _____ there when
        I called.

C. Write the questions.

Ex. We're arguing with <u>our landlord</u>.

    <u>Who are you arguing with?</u>

1. I'm writing about <u>my favorite movie</u>.

    _____

2. They're going to fix <u>their bookcase</u>.

    _____

3. He hiked <u>in the mountains</u>.

    _____

4. She'll be ready <u>in a few minutes</u>.

    _____

5. They arrived <u>by plane</u>.

    _____

6. We'll be staying until <u>Monday</u>.

    _____

7. She's going to hire <u>five</u> people.

    _____

D. Answer the questions.

Ex. What did your daughter do yesterday morning?

(do her homework) _____ She did her homework. _____

1. What's your sister doing today?

(adjust her satellite dish) _____

2. What does your brother do every evening?

(chat online) _____

3. What are you going to do next weekend?

(visit my mother-in-law) _____

4. What did Jack and Rick do yesterday afternoon?

(deliver groceries) _____

5. What was David doing when his children came home from school?

(bake a cake) _____

6. How will you get to work tomorrow?

(take the bus) _____

7. What will you and your husband be doing this evening?

(watch TV) _____

8. How did you cut your hand?

(chop carrots) _____

E. Listen to each question and then complete the answer.

Ex. Yes, _____ he does _____.

1. Yes, _____.   5. No, _____.

2. No, _____.   6. Yes, _____.

3. Yes, _____.   7. No, _____.

4. Yes, _____.   8. Yes, _____.

1. I ride horses.

   ___I've ridden___ horses for many years.

2. I fly airplanes.

   _____ airplanes for several years.

3. I give injections at the hospital.

   _____ injections for many years.

4. I speak Italian.

   _____ it all my life.

5. I take photographs.

   _____ them for many years.

6. I do exercises every day.

   _____ them every day for many years.

7. I draw cartoons.

   _____ cartoons for several years.

8. I write for a newspaper.

   _____ for a newspaper for many years.

9. I drive carefully.

   _____ carefully all my life.

B LISTENING

Listen and choose the word you hear.

1. a. ridden
   b. written

2. a. taking
   b. taken

3. a. giving
   b. given

4. a. written
   b. driven

5. a. writing
   b. written

6. a. drawing
   b. doing

7. a. spoken
   b. speaking

8. a. done
   b. drawn

be	fly	give	ride	sing	take
draw	get	go	see	swim	write

1. _____I've never flown_____
in a helicopter.

2. _____
a raise.

3. _____
in a limousine.

4. _____
a cartoon.

5. _____
a book.

6. _____
a trip to Hawaii.

7. _____
in a choir.

8. _____
in the Mediterranean.

9. _____
on television.

10. _____
on a cruise.

11. _____
a present to my teacher.

12. _____
a Broadway show.

D LISTENING

Is Speaker B answering *Yes* or *No*? Listen to each conversation and circle the correct answer.

1. (Yes)   No   3. Yes   No   5. Yes   No   7. Yes   No

2. Yes   No   4. Yes   No   6. Yes   No   8. Yes   No

fall	get	give	go	ride	wear

1. A. _____ *Have you ever gotten* _____ stuck in bad traffic?

   B. Yes. As a matter of fact, _____ *I got* _____ stuck in very bad traffic this morning.

2. A. _____ on a Ferris wheel?

   B. Yes, I have. _____ on a Ferris wheel last weekend.

3. A. _____ a tuxedo?

   B. Yes, I have. _____ a tuxedo to my sister's wedding.

4. A. _____ scuba diving?

   B. Yes, I have. _____ scuba diving last summer.

5. A. _____ blood?

   B. Yes, I have. _____ blood a few months ago.

6. A. _____ on the sidewalk?

   B. Yes. In fact, _____ on the sidewalk a few days ago.

F **GRAMMARRAP:** *Have You Ever?*

Listen. Then clap and practice.

A. Have you ever   seen   a rainbow?

   Have you ever   learned   to dance?

   Have you ever   flown   an airplane?

   Have you ever   gone   to France?

B. No, I've never   seen   a rainbow.

   I've never   learned   to dance.

   I've never   flown   an airplane.

   But I've often   gone   to France.

G **WHAT ARE THEY SAYING?**

drive	eat	go	meet	see	speak	take	write

1. A. __Have__ your children __eaten__ breakfast yet?

   B. Yes, __they have__ . __They ate__ breakfast a little while ago.

2. A. _____ George _____ his new car yet?

   B. Yes, _____ . _____ it for the first time this morning.

3. A. _____ Gloria _____ to the post office yet?

   B. Yes, _____ . _____ to the post office a little while ago.

4. A. _____ you and Jane _____ the new movie at the Westville Mall?

   B. Yes, _____ . _____ it last Saturday night.

5. A. _____ the employees _____ inventory yet?

   B. Yes, _____ . _____ inventory last weekend.

6. A. _____ you _____ to the landlord yet?

   B. Yes, _____ . _____ to him this morning.

7. A. _____ I _____ a letter to the Carter Company yet?

   B. Yes, _____ . _____ them a letter last week.

8. A. _____ you and your wife _____ your daughter's new boyfriend yet?

   B. Yes, _____ . _____ him last Friday night.

1. Kenji and his girlfriend aren't going to eat at Burger Town today. ___They've___ already

   ____eaten____ at Burger Town this week. ___They ate___ there on Monday.

2. My sister isn't going dancing tonight. _____ already _____ dancing this week.

   _____ dancing last night.

3. Timothy isn't going to wear his new jacket to work today. _____ already _____ it to

   work this week. _____ it yesterday.

4. My husband and I aren't going to do our laundry today. _____ already _____ our

   laundry this week. _____ it on Saturday.

5. Roger isn't going to give his girlfriend candy today. _____ already _____ her

   candy this week. _____ her candy yesterday morning.

6. I'm not going to see a movie today. _____ already _____ a movie this week.

   _____ a movie on Wednesday.

7. We aren't going to buy fruit at the supermarket today. _____ already _____

   fruit at the supermarket this week. _____ some fruit two days ago.

8. Susie isn't going to visit her grandparents today. _____ already _____

   them this week. _____ them yesterday.

9. David isn't going to take his children to the circus today. _____ already _____

   them to the circus this week. _____ them to the circus a few days ago.

go
went
gone

1. We should ____go____ now.

2. They ____went____ home early today.

3. She's already ____gone____ home.

see
saw
seen

4. I've never _____ him.

5. I _____ her yesterday.

6. Do you _____ them often?

eat
ate
eaten

7. I _____ there this morning.

8. Has he ever _____ there?

9. Do you _____ there every day?

write
wrote
written

10. How often do you _____ to them?

11. She's already _____ her report.

12. He _____ her a very long letter.

wear
wore
worn

13. When will you _____ it?

14. He's never _____ it.

15. She _____ it today.

speak
spoke
spoken

16. Who _____ to you about it?

17. She can't _____ Chinese.

18. Have they _____ to you?

drive
drove
driven

19. They've never _____ there.

20. We never like to _____ there.

21. She _____ there today.

do
did
done

22. Did you _____ your homework?

23. We _____ that yesterday.

24. Have you ever _____ that?

WHAT ARE THEY SAYING?

1. A. Janet, you've got to do your homework.

   B. But, Mother, __I've__ already _____ my homework today.

   A. Really? When?

   B. Don't you remember? _____ my homework this afternoon.

   A. Oh, that's right. Also, _____ you _____ a letter to Grandma yet?

   B. Yes, _____. I wrote to her yesterday.

2. A. Would you like to swim at the health club tonight?

   B. I don't think so. _____ already _____ at the health club today.

   A. Really? When?

   B. _____ there this morning.

3. A. Are you going to take your vitamins?

   B. _____ already _____ them.

   A. Really? When?

   B. _____ them before breakfast. How about you? _____ you _____ yours?

   A. Yes, _____. I _____ mine when I got up.

4. A. I hope Jimmy gets a haircut soon.

   B. Don't worry, Mother. _____ already _____ one.

   A. I'm glad to hear that. When?

   B. _____ a haircut yesterday.

   A. That's wonderful!

5. A. When are you and Fred going to eat at the new restaurant downtown?

B. _____ already _____ there.

A. Really? When?

B. _____ there last weekend.

A. How was the food?

B. It was terrible. It was the worst food we've ever _____!

6. A. When are you going to speak to the boss about a raise?

B. _____ already _____ to her.

A. Really? When?

B. _____ to her this morning.

A. What did she say?

B. She said, "_____."

Listen. Then clap and practice.

A. Have you gone to the   bank?

B.   Yes,   I have.

    I went to the   bank   at noon.

A. Have they taken   a vacation?

B.   Yes,   they have.

    They took   a vacation   in June.

A. Has he written   the letters?

B.   Yes,   he has.

    He wrote   the letters   today.

A. Has she gotten   a raise?

B.   Yes,   she has.

    She got   a raise   last May.

buy	dance	fly	go	read	see	swim
clean	eat	give	make	ride	study	take

1. A. What's the matter, Susan? You aren't riding very well today.

   B. I know. _____I haven't ridden_____ in a long time.

2. A. I can't believe it! These cars are very expensive.

   B. Remember, we _____ a new car in a long time.

3. A. Are you nervous?

   B. Yes, I am. _____ in an airplane in a long time.

4. A. Are you excited about your vacation?

   B. Yes, I am. _____ a vacation in a long time.

5. A. You aren't swimming very well today.

   B. I know. _____ in a long time.

6. A. Buster is really hungry.

   B. I know. He _____ anything in a long time.

7. A. Susie's room is very dirty.

   B. I know. She _____ it in a long time.

8. A. I think Timmy watches too much TV.

   B. You're right. _____ a book in a long time.

9. A. Mom, who was the sixteenth
   president of the United States?

   B. I'm not sure. _____
   American history in a long time.

10. A. Everyone says the new movie at the
    Center Cinema is excellent.

    B. Let's see it. We _____
    a good movie in a long time.

11. A. Are you nervous?

    B. Yes, I am. _____
    blood in a long time.

12. A. What's Dad doing?

    B. He's making dinner. _____
    dinner in a long time.

13. A. Is there any fruit in the refrigerator?

    B. No, there isn't. I _____
    to the supermarket in a long time.

14. A. Ouch!!

    B. Sorry. _____
    in a long time.

M PUZZLE: *What Have They Already Done?*

Across
1. wash
5. fly
8. go
10. explain
11. meet
12. take

Down
2. see
3. drive
4. play
6. wear
7. drink
8. get
9. be

Richard is going to have a party tonight, and he has a lot of things to do.

✔	go to the supermarket
☐	clean my apartment
✔	get a haircut
☐	bake a cake
✔	fix my CD player

1. _____He's already gone to the supermarket._____

2. _____He hasn't cleaned his apartment yet._____

3. _____

4. _____

5. _____

Susan is going to work this morning, and she has a lot of things to do.

✔	take a shower
☐	do my exercises
☐	feed the cat
✔	walk the dog
☐	eat breakfast

6. _____

7. _____

8. _____

9. _____

10. _____

Beverly and Paul are going on a trip tomorrow, and they have a lot of things to do.

☐	do our laundry
✔	get our paychecks
✔	pay our bills
☐	pack our suitcases
☐	say good-bye to our friends

11. _____

12. _____

13. _____

14. _____

15. _____

Roberta is very busy today.
She has a lot of things to
do at the office.

✔	write to Mrs. Lane
✔	call Mr. Sanchez
☐	meet with Ms. Wong
☐	read my e-mail
✔	send a fax to the Ace Company

16. _____

17. _____

18. _____

19. _____

20. _____

You have a lot of things to do today. What have you done? What haven't you done?

1. ....

2. ....

3. ....

4. ....

5. ....

LISTENING

What things have these people done? What haven't they done? Listen and check *Yes* or *No*.

		Yes	*No*			*Yes*	*No*
1.	do homework	✔	____	5.	do the laundry	____	____
	practice the violin	____	✔		vacuum the rugs	____	____
2.	write the report	____	____	6.	get the food	____	____
	send a fax	____	____		clean the house	____	____
3.	feed the dog	____	____	7.	speak to the landlord	____	____
	eat breakfast	____	____		call Ajax Electric	____	____
4.	fix the pipes	____	____	8.	hook up the VCR	____	____
	repair the washing machine	____	____		read the instructions	____	____

1. A. Have you spoken to David recently?

   B. Yes, I __have__ . I _____ to him last night.

   A. What _____ he say?

   B. He's worried because he's going to fly in a helicopter

      this week, and he's never _____ in a
      helicopter before.

2. A. _____ you seen any good movies recently?

   B. No, I _____ . I _____ a movie last week,
      but it was terrible.

   A. Really? What movie did you _____?

   B. _The Man from Madagascar._ It's one of the worst

      movies I've ever _____ .

3. A. I think I forgot to do something, but I can't remember
      what I forgot to do.

   B. Have you _____ the mail to the post office?

   A. Yes. I _____ it to the post office an hour ago.

   B. _____ you _____ a fax to the Ace Company?

   A. Yes. I _____ them a fax this morning.

   B. _____ you _____ the employees their
      paychecks?

   A. Uh-oh! That's what I forgot to do!

4. A. _____ you gone on vacation yet?

   B. Yes, I _____ . I _____ to Venice.
      It was phenomenal!

   A. _____ you ever _____ to Venice before?

   B. Yes, I _____ . I _____ there a few years
      ago.

5. A. What _____ you get for your birthday?

B. My family _____ me seventy-five dollars.

A. That's fantastic! What _____?

B. Going to buy? I've already _____ all my birthday money.

A. Really? What _____ buy?

B. I _____ a lot of CDs. Do you want to _____ to them?

6. A. Are you ready to leave soon?

B. No, _____. I haven't _____ a shower yet.

A. But you _____ up an hour ago. You're really slow today. _____ you eaten breakfast yet?

B. Of course _____. I _____ a little while ago, and I've already _____ the dishes.

A. Well, hurry up! It's 8:30. I don't want to be late.

Q LISTENING

Listen to each word and then say it.

j!

1. job
2. jacket
3. juice
4. jam
5. jog
6. pajamas
7. journalist
8. just
9. Jennifer

10. you
11. yoga
12. yellow
13. yard
14. yesterday
15. young
16. yogurt
17. yet
18. New York

y!

R JULIA'S BROKEN KEYBOARD

Julia's keyboard is broken. The j's and the y's don't always work.
Fill in the missing j's and y's and then read Julia's letters aloud.

1.

_J_udy,

    Have you seen my blue and
_y_ellow _j_acket at __our house?
I think I left it there __esterday
after the __azz concert. I've looked
everywhere, and I __ust can't find
it anywhere.

                       __ulia

2.

Dear __ennifer,

    We're sorry __ou haven't been able
to visit us this __ear. Do __ou think
__ou could come in __une or __uly?
We really en__oyed __our visit last
__ear. We really want to see __ou
again.

                       __ulia

3.

__eff,

    __ack and I have gone out __ogging,
but we'll be back in __ust a few
minutes. Make __ourself comfortable.
__ou can wait for us in the __ard. We
haven't eaten lunch __et. We'll have
some __ogurt and orange __uice when
we get back.

                       __ulia

4.

Dear __ane,

    We __ust received the beautiful
pa__amas __ou sent to __immy.
Thank __ou very much. __immy is
too __oung to write to __ou himself,
but he says "Thank __ou." He's
already worn the pa__amas, and
he's en__oying them a lot.

                       __ulia

5.

Dear __anet,

    __ack and I are coming to visit
__ou and __ohn in New __ork. We've
been to New __ork before, but we
haven't visited the Statue of Liberty
or the Empire State Building __et.
See __ou in __anuary or maybe in
__une.

                       __ulia

6.

Dear __oe,

    We got a letter from __ames last
week. He has en__oyed college a lot
this __ear. His favorite sub__ects
are German and __apanese. He's
looking for a __ob as a __ournalist
in __apan, but he hasn't found one
__et.

                       __ulia

IS OR HAS?

1. He's already eaten lunch.
   _____ is
   ✔ has

2. He's eating lunch.
   ✔ is
   _____ has

3. She's taking a bath.
   _____ is
   _____ has

4. She's taken a bath.
   _____ is
   _____ has

5. He's having a good time.
   _____ is
   _____ has

6. She's going to get up.
   _____ is
   _____ has

7. He's bought a lot of CDs recently.
   _____ is
   _____ has

8. It's snowing.
   _____ is
   _____ has

9. She's thirsty.
   _____ is
   _____ has

10. He's got to leave now.
    _____ is
    _____ has

11. Where's the nearest health club?
    _____ is
    _____ has

12. She's written the report.
    _____ is
    _____ has

13. He's taking a lot of photographs.
    _____ is
    _____ has

14. He's taken a few photographs.
    _____ is
    _____ has

15. He's spent all his money.
    _____ is
    _____ has

16. There's a library across the street.
    _____ is
    _____ has

17. She's gone kayaking.
    _____ is
    _____ has

18. It's very warm.
    _____ is
    _____ has

19. He's embarrassed.
    _____ is
    _____ has

20. This is the best book she's ever read.
    _____ is
    _____ has

A HOW LONG?

for	since

1.

   How long have you had a headache?

   I've had a headache

   ___since___ this morning.

2. How long have your parents been married?

   _____ a long time.

3. How long has your brother owned a motorcycle?

   _____ last summer.

4. How long has your sister been interested in astronomy?

   _____ several years.

5. How long have you had a cell phone?

   _____ last month.

6. How long have you and your husband known each other?

   _____ 1994.

7. How long have the Wilsons had a dog?

   _____ a few weeks.

8. How long have you had problems with your upstairs neighbor?

   _____ a year.

9. How long has your daughter been a computer programmer?

   _____ 2000.

10. How long has your son played in the school orchestra?

    _____ September.

11. How long have there been mice in your attic?

    _____ two months.

B WHAT'S THE QUESTION?

1. _____How long has_____ your daughter

_____wanted to be an engineer_____?

She's wanted to be an engineer for a long time.

2. _____ James

_____?

He's owned his own house since 2001.

3. _____ your grandparents

_____?

They've been married for 50 years.

4. _____ you

_____?

I've been interested in photography since last year.

5. _____ Gregory

_____?

He's worn glasses since last spring.

6. _____ your cousins

_____?

They've known how to snowboard for a few years.

7. _____ your son

_____?

He's had a girlfriend for several months.

8. _____ there

_____?

There's been a pizza shop in town since last fall.

C **GrammarRap:** *How Long Have You Known Maria?*

Listen. Then clap and practice.

A. How long have you   known   Maria?

B. I've known her   since I was   two.

A. Have you met   her older   sister?

B. No, I haven't.   Have you?

A. How long   has your son   been in college?

B. He's been there   since early   September.

A. Does he like   all of his   courses?

B. I think so.   I can't   remember.

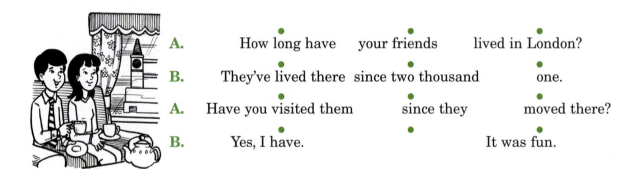

A. How long have   your friends   lived in London?

B. They've lived there since two thousand   one.

A. Have you visited them   since they   moved there?

B. Yes, I have.   It was fun.

A. How long has   your brother   been married?

B. He's been married   for seven   months.

A. Have you seen him   since   his wedding?

B. I've seen him   only   once.

1. _____I'm_____ sick today.

   _____I've been sick_____ since I got up this morning.

3. Roger _____ how to ski.

   _____ how to ski since he took lessons last winter.

5. _____ lost.

   _____ lost since we arrived here this morning.

7. _____ cold and cloudy.

   _____ cold and cloudy since we got here last weekend.

9. My boyfriend _____ bored.

   _____ bored since the concert began forty-five minutes ago.

2. Rita _____ a swollen knee.

   _____ a swollen knee since she played soccer last Saturday.

4. _____ nervous.

   _____ nervous since they got married a few hours ago.

6. I _____ a stiff neck.

   _____ a stiff neck since I went to a tennis match yesterday.

8. My daughter _____ the cello.

   _____ played the cello since she was six years old.

10. _____ afraid of dogs.

   _____ afraid of dogs since my neighbor's dog bit me last year.

Listen and choose the correct answer.

1. a. Bob is in the army.
   b. Bob is engaged. *(circled)*

2. a. Carol is in music school.
   b. Carol is a professional musician.

3. a. Michael has been home for a week.
   b. Michael hurt himself this week.

4. a. She hasn't started her new job.
   b. She gets up early every morning.

5. a. Richard is in college.
   b. Richard hasn't eaten in the cafeteria.

6. a. Nancy and Tom met five and a half years ago.
   b. Nancy and Tom met when they were five and a half years old.

7. a. They play soccer every weekend.
   b. They're eight years old.

8. a. Patty is a teenager.
   b. Patty has short hair.

9. a. Ron used to own his own business.
   b. Ron moved nine years ago.

10. a. She's interested in astronomy.
    b. She's eleven years old.

11. a. He's in high school.
    b. He isn't in high school now.

12. a. Alan has owned his house for fifteen years.
    b. Alan doesn't have problems with his house now.

F CROSSWORD

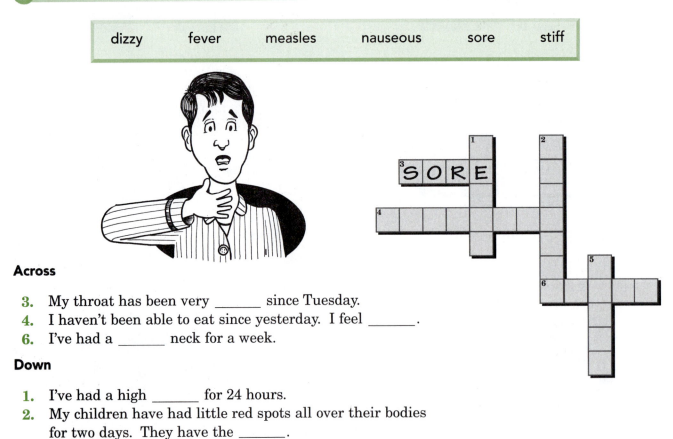

dizzy   fever   measles   nauseous   sore   stiff

Across

3. My throat has been very _____ since Tuesday.
4. I haven't been able to eat since yesterday. I feel _____ .
6. I've had a _____ neck for a week.

Down

1. I've had a high _____ for 24 hours.
2. My children have had little red spots all over their bodies for two days. They have the _____ .
5. I've been _____ since I fell down and hurt my head.

G SCRAMBLED SENTENCES

Unscramble the sentences.

1. she   a   jazz   Julie   liked   teenager.   has   was   since

   _____ Julie has liked jazz since she was a teenager. _____

2. he   play   little   the   since   known   a   boy.   He's   piano   was   how   to

   _____

3. since   I've   was   in   I   astronomy   young.   interested   been

   _____

4. since   been   they   college.   engaged   They've   finished

   _____

5. been   he   a   cooking   He's   graduated   from   chef   school.   since

   _____

6. she   wanted   be   to   teacher   eighteen   She's   a   years   since   old.   was

   _____

7. moved   ago.   business   They've   their   year   owned   since   a   they   here   own

   _____

H WRITE ABOUT YOURSELF

1. I'm interested in _____.

   I've been interested in _____ since _____.

2. I own _____.

   I've owned _____ since _____.

3. I like _____.

   I've _____ since _____.

4. I want to _____.

   I've _____ since _____.

5. I know how to _____.

   I've _____ since _____.

be	have	speak	teach	visit	walk

1. Mr. and Mrs. Miller __walk__ every day.

_____ every day since Mr. Miller had problems with his heart last

year. Before that, _____ never

_____. They stayed home and watched TV.

2. Sam _____ with a Boston accent.

_____ with a Boston accent since he moved to Boston last summer.

Before that, _____ with a New York accent.

3. Terry _____ a truck driver. She drives a truck between the east coast

and the west coast. _____ a truck driver for a year. Before that,

_____ a taxi driver.

4. Before he moved to Brazil, Professor Baker

_____ French. Now _____

English. _____ English at a Brazilian university for the past two years.

5. Your Uncle Walter _____ already

_____ us five times this year!

Last year, he _____ us only twice. How many times will he

_____ us next year?!

6. Tiffany _____ long blonde hair.

_____ long blonde hair since she became a movie star. Before that, she

_____ short brown hair. Tiffany looks very different now!

Victor
(be)

musician   1990–now
photographer   1982–1989

Mrs. Sanchez
(teach)

science   1995–now
math   1985–1994

my grandparents
(have)

dog   1998–now
cat   1986–1997

Betty
(work)

bank   2000–now
mall   1997–1999

my parents
(live)

Miami   2001–now
New York   1980–2000

1. How long _____ *has Victor been* _____ a musician?

   _____ *He's been a musician* _____ since _____ *1990* _____ .

2. How long _____ *was he* _____ a photographer?

   _____ *He was a photographer* _____ for _____ *7 years* _____ .

3. How long _____ science?

   _____ since _____ .

4. How long _____ math?

   _____ for _____ .

5. How long _____ a cat?

   _____ for _____ .

6. How long _____ a dog?

   _____ since _____ .

7. How long _____ at the bank?

   _____ since _____ .

8. How long _____ at the mall?

   _____ for _____ .

9. How long _____ in New York?

   _____ for _____ .

10. How long _____ in Miami?

    _____ since _____ .

1. Do you still go skiing every winter?

No. ....
.... (for/since) ....
....

2. Do you still live ....
.... ?

No. ....
.... (for/since) ....
....

3. Are you still a/an ....
.... ?

No. ....
.... (for/since) ....
....

4. How long have you been interested in
.... ?

....
.... (for/since) ....
....

5. Do you still ....
....
in your free time?

No. ....
.... (for/since) ....
....

6. Do your brothers still call you "Tiny Tim"?

No. ....

.... (for/since) ....

....

7. How long have you ....

....

....................?

....

.... (for/since) ....

....

8. Do you still ....

....

....................?

No. ....

.... (for/since) ....

....

L LISTENING

Listen and choose the correct answer.

1. a. He's always been a salesperson.
    b. He was a cashier.

2. a. His daughter was in medical school.
    b. His daughter is in medical school.

3. a. Her parents haven't always lived in a house.
    b. Her parents have always lived in a house.

4. a. He's always wanted to be an actor.
    b. He isn't in college now.

5. a. They exercise at their health club every day.
    b. They haven't exercised at their health club since last year.

6. a. James hasn't always been a bachelor.
    b. James has been married for ten years.

7. a. Jane has wanted to meet a writer.
    b. Jane wants to be a writer.

8. a. He's never broken his ankle.
    b. He's never sprained his ankle.

9. a. She's always liked rock music.
    b. She hasn't always liked classical music.

10. a. Billy has had a fever for two days.
    b. Billy has had a sore throat for two days.

11. a. Jennifer has always been the manager.
    b. Jennifer hasn't been a salesperson since last fall.

12. a. He's interested in modern art now.
    b. He's always been interested in art.

A   WHAT'S THE WORD?

| for | since |

1. We've been living here __since__ 2001.

2. It's been raining _____ two days.

3. I've been listening to this CD _____ an hour.

4. She's been flying airplanes _____ 1995.

5. Billy, you've been roller-blading _____ this morning!

6. He's been practicing the cello _____ three and a half hours.

7. Our neighbors have been vacuuming

   _____ 7 A.M.

8. We've been having problems with our

   heat _____ a week.

B   CHOOSE

1. I've been working here since _____.
   a. last month *(circled)*
   b. three months

2. He's been taking a shower for _____.
   a. this afternoon
   b. half an hour

3. It's been ringing for _____.
   a. two o'clock
   b. a few minutes

4. She's been studying since _____.
   a. eight o'clock
   b. an hour

5. They've been dating for _____.
   a. high school
   b. six months

6. I've been feeling sick since _____.
   a. twelve hours
   b. yesterday

1. How long have you been studying?

   _____I've been studying since_____
   early this morning.

3. How long has Tom been having problems with his car?

   _____
   a week.

5. How long have we been waiting?

   _____
   forty-five minutes.

7. How long has Professor Drake been talking?

   _____
   an hour and a half.

9. How long have you been teaching?

   _____
   1975.

2. How long has Ann been feeling sick?

   _____
   a few days.

4. How long have the people next door been arguing?

   _____
   last night.

6. How long has that cell phone been ringing?

   _____
   the play began.

8. How long have Rick and Sally been dating?

   _____
   high school.

10. How long have I been chatting online?

    _____
    more than two hours.

D WHAT ARE THEY DOING?

assemble	bake	bark	browse	do	jog	look	make	plant

1. Larry _____is looking_____ for his keys.

   _____He's been looking_____ for his keys all morning.

2. My sister _____ in the park.

   _____ in the park since 8 A.M.

3. The dog next door _____.

   _____ all day.

4. Our neighbors _____ flowers.

   _____ flowers for several hours.

5. Michael _____ his homework.

   _____ his homework since dinner.

6. My wife _____ the web.

   _____ the web for an hour.

7. Mr. and Mrs. Lee _____ their son's new bicycle.

   _____ it all afternoon.

8. I'm _____ cookies.

   _____ cookies since two o'clock.

9. You and your brother _____ a lot of noise!

   _____ noise since you got up.

E LISTENING

Listen and choose the correct time expressions to complete the sentences.

1. (a.) 1995.
   b. a few years.

2. a. 1:45.
   b. forty-five minutes.

3. a. 3 o'clock.
   b. thirty minutes.

4. a. yesterday.
   b. several days.

5. a. 7:30 this morning.
   b. more than an hour.

6. a. 7 o'clock.
   b. a half hour.

7. a. a few weeks.
   b. last month.

8. a. about three hours.
   b. 4 o'clock.

9. a. early this morning.
   b. twenty minutes.

Listen. Then clap and practice.

A.   How long have you been   working   at the mall?

B.   I've been working   at the mall   since the fall.

A.   How long has she been   wearing   her new ring?

B.   She's been wearing   her new ring   since the spring.

A.   How long have you been   living   in L.A.?

B.   We've been living   in L.A.   since May.

A.   How long has he been   waiting   for the train?

B.   He's been waiting   since it started   to rain.

A.   How long have you been   looking for   that mouse?

B.   We've been looking   since we rented   this house.

make	play	run	snow	study	take	vacuum	wait	wear	work

1. Excuse me.

   <u>Have you been waiting</u> in line for a long time?

   Yes, I <u>have</u>.

   <u>I've been waiting</u> for more than an hour.

2. What a terrible day! _____ for a long time?

   Yes, _____. _____ since early this morning.

3. Your son plays the violin very beautifully. _____ lessons for a long time?

   Yes, _____. _____ lessons since he was five.

4. _____ here for a long time?

   No, _____. I've _____ here for only a week.

5. _____ your car _____ strange noises for a long time?

   Yes, _____. _____ these noises all week.

6. You look tired. _____ for a long time?

   Yes, _____. _____ all morning.

7. Your children speak French very well.

_____ it for a long time?

Yes, _____.

_____ French for six years.

8. I'm really tired.

_____ for a long time?

Yes, we _____.

_____ since 6 A.M.

9. Your pants are dirty.

_____ them all week?

No, _____.

_____ them for only a few hours.

10. This is the sixth game you've won today.

_____ for a long time?

No, _____.

_____ for only a few months.

H LISTENING

Listen and choose what the people are talking about.

1. a. traffic
   b. a computer

2. a. a wall
   b. the furniture

3. a. the guitar
   b. my bills

4. a. the drums
   b. tennis

5. a. the cookies
   b. the babies

6. a. the cake
   b. the bridge

7. a. her composition
   b. her bicycle

8. a. books
   b. trains

9. a. a sandwich
   b. a novel

10. a. socks
    b. chairs

11. a. the president
    b. CDs

12. a. a restaurant
    b. a neighbor

13. a. fruit
    b. my car

14. a. a test
    b. a cake

15. a. videos
    b. problems

Listen to each word and then say it.

| th**i**s |

| 1. b**i**lls | 3. ch**i**cken | 5. b**ui**lding |
| 2. off**i**cer | 4. t**i**cket | 6. **i**tself |

| th**e**se |

| 1. w**ee**k | 3. br**ie**fcase | 5. f**e**ver |
| 2. sp**ea**k | 4. fr**ie**ndly | 6. **ea**ten |

Listen and put a circle around the word that has the same sound.

1. th**i**n:	pol**i**ce	t**i**red	(**i**nterested)
2. b**ui**ld:	h**ea**dache	**i**s	sw**ea**ter
3. r**ea**d:	St**e**ve's	b**ee**n	tr**y**
4. **i**f:	**i**n	b**i**te	tax**i**
5. l**i**ve:	m**e**t	h**i**story	ch**i**ld
6. f**i**shing:	sc**i**ence	wr**i**ting	s**i**ster
7. p**ie**ce:	ver**y**	w**ea**r	w**i**nter
8. **ea**st:	h**i**re	Chin**e**se	r**ea**dy

Now make a sentence using all the words you circled, and read the sentence aloud.

9. ....

10. k**ey**:	d**i**nner	rec**ei**ve	th**i**nk
11. tenn**i**s:	**ea**sy	h**ea**ter	th**i**s
12. complet**e**:	an**y**	g**e**t	tr**y**
13. k**ee**p:	b**u**sy	P**e**ter	d**i**sturb
14. tux**e**do:	t**y**pe	**i**f	w**ee**k
15. L**i**nda:	d**i**dn't	gr**ee**n	br**i**ght
16. m**ee**ting:	ch**i**ld	forg**e**t	**e**-mail

Now make a sentence using all the words you circled, and read the sentence aloud.

17. ....

YOU DECIDE: *What Have They Been Doing?*

1. I have a sore throat.

No wonder you have a sore throat!

You've been singing all day.

2. My back hurts.

No wonder your back hurts!

_____ all day.

3. Bob has a terrible sunburn.

No wonder he has a terrible sunburn!

_____ all day.

4. Nancy is very tired.

No wonder she's very tired!

_____ all day.

5. Jane and I have headaches.

No wonder you have headaches!

_____ all day.

6. Bob and Judy are very disappointed.

No wonder they're very disappointed!

_____ all day.

7. I can't finish my dinner.

No wonder you can't finish your dinner!

_____ all day.

8. Victor doesn't have any money.

No wonder he doesn't have any money!

_____ all day.

complain	eat	go	make	read	see	study	swim	talk	write

1. My husband and I are very full. ___We've been eating___ for the

past two hours. __We've__ already ____eaten____ soup, salad,

chicken, and vegetables. And our dinner isn't finished.

___We haven't eaten___ our dessert yet!

2. Dr. Davis is tired. _____ patients since early

this morning. _____ already _____ twenty patients,

and it's only two o'clock. _____ the other
patients in her waiting room yet.

3. Dave likes to swim. _____ for an hour

and a half. _____ already _____ across the pool thirty
times.

4. Amy is very tired. _____ to job interviews for

the past three weeks. _____ already _____ to ten job

interviews, and she hasn't found a job yet!

5. Gregory loves to talk. _____ all evening.

_____ already _____ about his job, his house, and his

car. Fortunately, _____ about his cats yet.

6. Betty and Bob are writing thank-you notes for their wedding gifts,

and they're very tired. _____ them all weekend.

_____ already _____ to their aunts, uncles, and

cousins, but _____ to their friends yet.

7. Andrew is tired. He's having a party tonight, and _____

_____ desserts since early this morning.

_____ already _____ two apple pies and three

blueberry pies. But he isn't finished. _____

a chocolate cake yet.

8. Patty is very tired. _____ since she got home

from school. _____ already _____ English and math.

And she'll be up late tonight because _____
for her history test yet.

9. Today is Howard's day off, and he's enjoying himself. _____

_____ since early this morning. _____ already

_____ three short stories. But _____

today's newspaper yet.

10. Mr. and Mrs. Grumble like to complain. _____

all evening. _____ already _____ about their jobs, the
weather, and several members of their family. Fortunately, they

_____ about the party yet, but I'm sure they will.

L LISTENING

Listen and decide where the conversation is taking place.

1. a. in a kitchen
    b. in a supermarket

2. a. at home
    b. in school

3. a. in a department store
    b. in a laundromat

4. a. at a movie theater
    b. at home

5. a. at a clinic
    b. at a bakery

6. a. in a cafeteria
    b. in a library

7. a. at a concert hall
    b. at a museum

8. a. at a health club
    b. in a book store

9. a. in an office
    b. at a bus stop

10. a. at a zoo
    b. in a pet shop

11. a. at home
    b. at a movie theater

12. a. at a clinic
    b. in a department store

1. The floor is wet! How long has the ceiling been (leaking) / leaked ?

2. I'm not nervous. I've been flown / flying in helicopters for years.

3. I'm a little worried. I've never been running / run in a marathon before.

4. How many pizzas have you already made / been making so far today?

5. You look tired. What have you / have you been doing today?

6. I think I've seen / been seeing this movie before.

7. Has your husband already giving / given blood?

8. I've never taken / been taking a karate lesson. Have you?

9. Have you ever been going / gone out on a date before?

10. Alexander, your cell phone has rung / has been ringing since we started class!

11. Jane isn't nervous. She's been sung / singing in front of audiences for years.

N YOU DECIDE: *What Are They Saying?*

A. Mrs. Vickers, could I speak to you for a few minutes?

B. Of course. Please sit down.

A. Mrs. Vickers, I've been thinking. I've been working here at the

_____ Company (for/since) _____ .
I've worked very hard, and I've done a lot of things here.

For example, I've _____ ,

I've _____ ,

and I've been _____

(for/since) _____ .

B. That's true, Mr. Mills. And we're happy with your work.

A. Thank you, Mrs. Vickers. As I was saying, I know I've done a very good job here, and I really think I should get a raise.

I haven't had a raise (for/since) _____ .

B. _____ .

A. _____ .

A. Dad, could I speak to you for a few minutes?

B. Sure, James. Please sit down.

A. Dad, I've been thinking. I've been working very hard in school this year, and I've done all my chores at home. For example,

I've _____ , I've _____

_____ , and I've been _____

_____ (for/since) _____ .

B. That's true, James. Your mother and I are very proud of you.

A. Thank you, Dad. As I was saying, I know I've been very responsible, and I really think I should be able to take your car when I go out on a date. After all, I've been driving

(for/since) _____ .

B. _____ .

A. _____ .

Daniel has been living in a small town in Mexico all his life. His father just got a good job in the United States, and Daniel and his family are going to live there. Daniel's life is going to be very different in the United States.

1. He's going to live in a big city.
2. He's going to take English lessons.
3. He's going to take the subway.
4. He's going to shop in American supermarkets.
5. He's going to eat American food.
6. He's going to play American football.

7. He's going to _____ .

Daniel is a little nervous.

1. _____ *He's never lived in a big city* _____ before.

2. _____ before.

3. _____ before.

4. _____ before.

5. _____ before.

6. _____ before.

7. .... before.

Daniel's cousins have been living in the United States for many years. They'll be able to help him.

8. _____ *They've been living in a big city* _____ for years.

9. _____ for years.

10. _____ for years.

11. _____ for years.

12. _____ for years.

13. _____ for years.

14. .... for years.

Daniel's cousins tell him he shouldn't worry. They're sure he'll enjoy his new life in the United States very much.

YOU DECIDE: *A New Life*

_____ has been living in _____

all her life. Now she's going to move to _____.
                                              (your city)

Her life is going to be very different in _____.
                                              (your city)

1. She's going to _____.

2. She's going to _____.

3. She's going to _____.

4. She's going to _____.

5. She's going to _____.

_____ is a little nervous.

6. _____ before.

7. _____ before.

8. _____ before.

9. _____ before.

10. _____ before.

_____ (has/have) been living in _____ for many
years and will be able to help her.

11. _____ for years.

12. _____ for years.

13. _____ for years.

14. _____ for years.

15. _____ for years.

_____ shouldn't worry. I'm sure she'll enjoy her new life in _____
very much.

A.   Complete the sentences with the present perfect.

Ex. *(do)*   Julie ___has___ already ___done___ her homework.

       (read)   I ___haven't read___ your report yet.

(eat)   **1.** Mary and her brother _____ already _____ breakfast.

(take)   **2.** My nephew _____ his violin lesson yet.

(write)   **3.** I _____ to my grandparents yet.

(go)   **4.** My wife _____ already _____ to work.

(pay)   **5.** You _____ your electric bill yet.

(have)   **6.** Henry _____ already _____ a problem with his new cell phone.

B.   Complete the questions.

1. A. _____ to your supervisor yet?

    B. Yes, I have. I spoke to her this morning.

2. A. _____ his new bicycle yet?

    B. Yes, he has. He rode it this morning.

3. A. _____ their paychecks yet?

    B. Yes, they have. They got them this afternoon.

4. A. _____ ever _____ in a helicopter?

    B. Yes, he has. He flew in a helicopter last summer.

5. A. _____ ever _____ on TV?

    B. Yes, she has. She was on TV last week.

6. A. _____ your daughter's new boyfriend yet?

    B. No, I haven't. I'm going to meet him tonight.

C.   Complete the sentences.

Ex. My neck is very stiff. _____It's been_____ stiff since I got up this morning.

       Tom is reading his e-mail. ___He's been reading___ it for a half hour.

1. It's sunny. _____ all week.

2. We're browsing the web. _____ the web since 8 o'clock.

3. My daughter has a fever. _____ a fever since early this morning.

4. My son is studying. _____ since he got home from school.

5. Our neighbors are arguing. _____ all afternoon.

6. I know how to skate. _____ how to skate since I was six years old.

7. Susan is interested in science. _____ interested in science since she was a teenager.

8. My husband and I are cleaning our basement. _____ it all weekend.

D. **Complete the answers.**

for	since

1. How long has your wife been working at the bank?

_____ 1999.

2. How long have those dogs been barking?

_____ a long time.

3. How long has it been snowing?

_____ two days.

4. How long have you wanted to be an astronaut?

_____ I was six years old.

E. **Complete the sentences.**

1. My brother owns a motorcycle. _____ a motorcycle since last summer.

Before that, _____ a bicycle.

2. I'm a journalist. _____ a journalist since 2000.

Before that, _____ an actor.

3. My daughter likes classical music. _____ classical music since she finished college.

Before that, _____ rock music.

F. **Listen and choose the correct answer.**

1. a. Janet is in acting school.
b. Janet is an actress.

2. a. The president has finished his speech.
b. The president is still speaking.

3. a. They've been living in New York since 1995.
b. They haven't lived in New York since 1995.

4. a. They're going to eat later.
b. They're going to eat now.

5. a. She's called the superintendent.
b. She has to call the superintendent.

6. a. Someone is helping Billy with his homework.
b. No one is helping Billy with his homework.

A WHAT DO THEY { ENJOY DOING / LIKE TO DO } ?

| enjoy _____ing | like to _____ | _____ing |

1. My wife and I _____enjoy_____ relaxing on the beach when we go on vacation.

2. Mrs. Finn is very talkative. She _____likes to_____ talk about her grandchildren.

   _____Talking_____ about her grandchildren is important to her.

3. Billy doesn't _____ going to the doctor, but he went yesterday for his annual checkup.

4. I _____ knit sweaters. _____ sweaters is a good way to relax.

5. My husband doesn't _____ asking for a raise, but sometimes he has to.

6. Dr. Brown _____ deliver babies. In her opinion, _____ babies is the best job in the world.

7. Bob doesn't _____ being a bachelor. He thinks _____ married is better.

8. Ann _____ plant flowers. She thinks _____ flowers is good exercise.

9. Jim _____ chatting online with his friends, but his parents think _____ online every evening isn't a very good idea.

10. Tom doesn't _____ play hockey. He thinks _____ hockey is dangerous.

11. My parents go to the gym during the winter, but in the summer they _____ going hiking.

12. Martin _____ go to parties. He thinks _____ to parties is a good way to meet people.

13. I really want to play the piano well, but I don't _____ practicing.

Listen. Then clap and practice.

Writing is   fun.

I like to   write.

I enjoy   writing letters   late   at night.

Eating is   fun.

I like to   eat.

I enjoy eating   fish,   and I like eating   meat.

Skiing is   great.

He likes to   ski.

But skiing's been   hard   since he hurt   his knee.

Singing is   fun.

She likes to   sing.

But today   she's sick,   and she can't sing   a thing.

Running is   great.

They like to   run.

Swimming's   okay,   but running's   more fun.

Baking is   great.

He likes to   bake.

When he's feeling   sad,   he bakes   a cake.

Knitting is   fun.

She likes to   knit.

She enjoys knitting   sweaters,   but none of them   fit!

C WHAT'S THE WORD?

clean	complain	eat	go	sit	wear
cleaning	complaining	eating	going	sitting	wearing

1. I hate to _____complain_____, but your loud music is disturbing me.

2. Carol tries to avoid _____ in the sun.

3. Sally likes to _____ dinner at home.

4. My son hates to _____ his room.

5. Richard can't stand to _____ a tie.

6. Tom avoids _____ his apartment whenever he can.

7. James doesn't like to _____ to the mall.

8. My husband and I hate _____ sailing.

9. My wife and I like to _____ in the park on a sunny day.

10. Please try to avoid _____ about the weather all the time.

11. My friends and I can't stand _____ in fast-food restaurants.

12. My daughter likes _____ the sweater you gave her for her birthday.

D GRAMMARRAP: *Pet Peeves*

Listen. Then clap and practice.

I don't like	waiting	for the bus	in the rain.
I hate to	rush	when I'm late	for a plane.
I avoid	talking	to strangers	on the train.
I can't stand	driving	in the center	lane.

I don't like to	iron	on a hot	summer day.
I hate to clean	the house	in the middle	of May.
I avoid	dusting	and sweeping	my floors.
I can't stand	doing	all my household	chores!

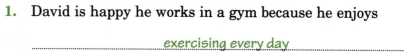

E YOU DECIDE: *What's the Reason?*

1. David is happy he works in a gym because he enjoys

   exercising every day .

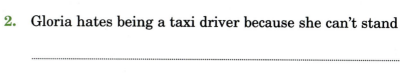

2. Gloria hates being a taxi driver because she can't stand

   ....

3. Miguel is glad he lives in Puerto Rico because he likes

   ....

4. I'm sorry I'm a secretary because I can't stand

   ....

5. We're happy we're going camping because we enjoy

   ....

6. William is upset he's sick because he hates

   ....

7. I'm glad I have a new bicycle because I like

   ....

8. Norman doesn't like being on a diet because he can't stand

   ....

9. Julie is happy she's a Hollywood actress because she enjoys

   ....

F MY ENERGETIC GRANDFATHER

A. Your grandfather is very energetic!

B. He sure is!

A. When did he start _____¹ the drums?

B. Believe it or not, he learned _____² the drums when he was sixty years old!

A. That's incredible! Does he _____³ the drums often?

B. Yes, he does. He's played every day for the last eight years.

A. What else does he enjoy doing?

B. He enjoys _____⁴, he enjoys _____⁵,

and he also enjoys _____⁶.

A. I hope I have that much energy when I'm his age!

G I CAN'T STAND IT!

I spoke with my friend Pam last weekend, and she talked a lot about figure skating. Ever since she started to figure skate several months ago, that's all she ever talks about! I never go out with her anymore because she practices figure skating all the time. And whenever I talk to her on the phone, figure skating is the only thing she talks about! (She thinks that everybody should learn to figure skate.) I can't stand it! I don't ever want to hear another word about figure skating!

Now YOU tell about somebody.

I spoke to my friend _____ last weekend, and _____ talked a lot about

_____ . Ever since _____

_____

_____

_____

_____ .

1. I've decided [buy / buying / (to buy)] a motorcycle.

4. You should consider [to change / change / changing] jobs.

2. Have you ever considered [to move / moving / move] ?

5. Have you decided to [get / to get / getting] a dog?

3. I'm thinking about [going / to go / go] on a diet.

6. He's thought about [to retire / retiring / retire] .

I **GRAMMARRAP:** *I Considered Ordering the Cheesecake*

Listen. Then clap and practice.

I considered   ordering the cheesecake.

Everyone   said I should   try it.

But then   I decided   to skip   dessert.

I wanted to   stay   on my diet.

I thought about   going   home early.

It was only   a quarter to   ten.

But I changed   my mind and   decided to   stay

When the music   started   again.

I thought about   moving to   France

And studying   music and   dance.

But I changed   my mind and   decided to   stay

With my cat   and my bird and my   plants.

A. Hi, Carla. How are you? We haven't spoken in a long time. Tell me, what have you been doing?

B. _____ .

A. Oh. And what are you thinking about doing after you finish studying English?

B. For a while, I considered _____ ,

and then I thought about _____ .

But I finally decided to _____ .

A. Oh. Why did you decide to do that?

B. Because _____ .

A. That's interesting. Tell me, Carla, have you ever considered _____

_____ ?

B. Yes. I thought about doing that, but decided it wasn't a very good idea.

A. Why not?

B. Because _____ .

A. Oh, I see.

B. So, Kathy, do you think I'm making the right decision?

A. _____ .

B. Do you really think so?

A. _____ .

B. Well, it was great talking to you. Let's get together soon.

A. Okay. I'll call you and we'll make some plans.

K WHAT'S THE WORD?

1. You can't keep on ____rearranging____ the furniture so often. You rearranged it last weekend!

2. I stopped _____ meat. I only eat fish and chicken.

3. He tried to quit _____, but he couldn't. He still worries about everything.

4. Alice always gets up late. She should start _____ up earlier.

5. Richard doesn't exercise very often. He should begin _____ every day. He'll feel a lot better.

6. You can't continue _____ me the same question. You've already asked me ten times!

7. I realize that I can't keep on _____ with people. I'm never going to argue with anyone again!

8. I know that Dave takes piano lessons. When did he start _____ guitar lessons?

9. You should stop _____ your bills late and start _____ them on time.

10. Professor Blaine is very boring. Students continue _____ asleep in his classes.

L GOOD DECISIONS

bite	clean	cook	do	gossip	interrupt	make	pay

This year I'm going to break all my bad habits. First, I've decided to stop ___biting___ [1] my nails. I've also started _____ [2] exercises every day. I learned _____ [3] when I was young, so I've decided to start _____ [4] healthy meals. I'm also considering _____ [5] my bills on time, and I'm thinking about _____ [6] my apartment every week. I've also decided to stop _____ [7] about other people and to stop _____ [8] my friends while they're talking.

1.

My husband can't stop _____falling_____ asleep at the movies. Every time we go, he falls asleep. If he keeps on _____ asleep, I'll never go to a movie with him again.

2.

I don't think I should continue _____ weights every day. I like _____ weights, but I'm afraid I might hurt my back if I keep on _____ them so often.

3.

My older sister always teases me. Today I'm really mad! She began _____ me early this morning, and she hasn't stopped. If she keeps on _____ me, I'm going to cry. And I won't stop _____ until she stops _____ me!

4.

My friend Albert has got to stop _____ so fast and start _____ more carefully. If he continues _____ fast, I'm sure he'll have a serious accident some day.

5.

Mr. Perkins, when are you going to stop _____ so sloppily and start _____ more neatly? If you keep on _____ like that, I'm going to have to fire you.

6.

My boyfriend is very clumsy. When we go dancing, he keeps on _____ on my feet. If he doesn't start _____ more gracefully, I'm going to stop _____ dancing with him.

LISTENING

Listen and choose the correct answer.

1. a. delivering babies. *(circled)*
   b. fix broken legs.

2. a. eating junk food.
   b. to pay our bills late.

3. a. swimming.
   b. to play golf.

4. a. to tap dance.
   b. figure skating.

5. a. to work out at a health club every week.
   b. retiring.

6. a. taking karate lessons.
   b. mend my pants.

7. a. to go back to college?
   b. moving?

8. a. to argue with people.
   b. biting my nails.

9. a. teasing your sister?
   b. to go to bed so late?

10. a. eat fruits and vegetables.
    b. worrying about my health all the time.

11. a. stand in line.
    b. wearing a suit.

12. a. taking photographs?
    b. study the piano?

13. a. to assemble his VCR.
    b. clean his apartment.

14. a. studying engineering.
    b. teach a computer course.

15. a. to live at home.
    b. going to school for the rest of your life.

O **WHAT DOES IT MEAN?**

Choose the correct answer.

1. My wife is very dizzy.
   a. I'm glad to hear that.
   b. How long has she been feeling sick? *(circled)*
   c. I guess she has a lot of things to do.

2. Peter and Nancy are vegetarians.
   a. They've quit eating vegetables.
   b. They've stopped planting flowers.
   c. They've stopped eating meat.

3. Andrew avoids talking about politics.
   a. He doesn't like talking about politics.
   b. He enjoys talking about politics.
   c. He's learning to talk about politics.

4. Shirley has worked her way to the top.
   a. She's the tallest person in her family.
   b. She's the president of her company.
   c. She works on the top floor of her building.

5. The people across the street were furious.
   a. They were embarrassed.
   b. They were awkward.
   c. They were very angry.

6. What's your present occupation?
   a. What do you do now?
   b. What are you going to do?
   c. What did you do when you were young?

7. This is my father-in-law, Mr. Kramer.
   a. He just graduated from high school.
   b. He just retired.
   c. He's seventeen years old.

8. My mother is going to mend my socks.
   a. She's going to fix them.
   b. She's going to wash them.
   c. She's going to send them to my sister.

9. You should stop gossiping.
   a. You should stop interrupting people.
   b. You should stop bumping into people.
   c. You should stop talking about people.

10. I've decided to ask for a raise.
    a. You should speak to your landlord.
    b. You should speak to your boss.
    c. You should speak to your instructor.

11. Dr. Wu has a lot of patients.
    a. That's true. She never gets angry.
    b. I know. She's a very popular doctor.
    c. That's true. She never gets sick.

12. My Uncle Gino has an Italian accent.
    a. He bought it when he went to Italy.
    b. He wears it all the time.
    c. Everybody knows he's from Italy.

1. Lisa didn't feel very well when she got up this morning because

   she *(eat)* ____had____ ____eaten____ a lot of candy before she went to bed.

2. My husband invited his boss for dinner last Friday night, and he forgot to tell me.

   Unfortunately, I *(get)* _____ already _____ tickets for a concert.

3. Our friends didn't stop showing us pictures of their grandson all evening. They

   (visit) _____ just _____ him the day before.

4. I wanted to drive to the mountains with my friends yesterday, but they *(drive)* _____

   _____ to the mountains the afternoon before.

5. Andrew wasn't very happy when I visited him yesterday. He *(cut)* _____ just _____
   himself while he was cooking dinner.

6. Alice couldn't buy the new printer she wanted because she *(spend)* _____ _____
   all her money on her vacation.

7. When my son got home from his date last night, my wife and I *(go)* _____ already

   _____ to sleep.

8. My children didn't want to eat pancakes for breakfast yesterday morning because

   I *(make)* _____ _____ pancakes the morning before.

9. I didn't see a movie with my friends last weekend because I *(see)* _____ _____
   three movies the weekend before.

10. When I got up this morning, my wife *(leave)* _____ already _____ for work.

11. Norman was upset when I saw him yesterday morning. He *(have)* _____ _____
    a big argument with his next-door neighbor the night before.

12. When I saw Jill today, she was very happy. Her boyfriend *(give)* _____ just _____
    her a beautiful bracelet for her birthday.

13. Tom couldn't lend me his dictionary the other day because he *(lose)* _____ _____
    it the week before.

Listen. Then clap and practice.

She felt very   happy   when she left   the store.
She had never   bought   a computer   before.

He looked   very nervous when he knocked   on the door.
He had never   gone out   on a date   before.

She felt very   weak,   and her throat was   sore.
She had never   had   the flu   before.

He felt   very proud   when his guests asked for   more.
He had never   baked   a pie   before.

She felt   very foolish   when her food   hit the floor.
She had never   eaten   with chopsticks   before.

He looked   very scared   when it started to   roar.
He had never   been close   to a lion   before.

She was very   annoyed   when he started to   snore.
He had never   made   so much noise   before.

He was very   surprised   when he opened   the drawer.
He had never   seen   so much money   before.

Gary Gray was very upset yesterday. He didn't get up until 9:00, and as a result, he was late for everything all day!

Today's meeting begins at 10:00.

2. He drove to the office and arrived late for an important meeting.

It _____ already _____.

Bank Closes at 3:00.

4. He got to the bank at 3:15, but he was too late. It _____ already _____.

To: garyg@go.com
From: tom@hopmail.com

I'll be leaving at 4:30. Hope to see you before then.

6. He had made plans to get together with his friend Tom. But he didn't get to Tom's office until 5:00. His friend Tom

_____ already _____.

Last train to Centerville leaves at 9:30.

1. He got to the train station at 9:45. The train ___had___ already _____left_____.

To: garyg@go.com
From: janet@hopmail.com

Let's have lunch at 12:00. I have to go back to work at 12:45.

3. He got to the restaurant at 1:00 to meet his friend Janet for lunch. However, she

_____ already _____ back to work.

Professor Tweedle's Lecture on Bird-Watching Starts at 4:00.

5. He got to the bird-watching lecture at 4:15. It _____ already _____.

Dear Gary,
    Our plane will be arriving at the airport at 8:10. We're looking forward to seeing you.
            Love,
            Grandma & Grandpa

7. He drove to the airport to pick up his grandmother and grandfather. He got to the airport at 8:30. Their plane

_____ already _____.

1. We got lost on the way to the party last night. We *(listen)* ____hadn't____ ____listened____ very carefully to the directions.

2. I enjoyed seeing my old friends at my high school reunion last weekend.

   I *(see)* _____ _____ them since we finished high school.

3. My wife and I decided to have a picnic in the park last Sunday. We *(have)* _____

   _____ a picnic in the park in a long time.

4. I went dancing with my girlfriend last Saturday night, and I hurt my back.

   I *(go)* _____ _____ dancing in a long time.

5. Cynthia was embarrassed at her party last night. She had invited her cousin Charles, but

   she *(remember)* _____ _____ to invite his girlfriend, Louise.

6. Frank looked terrible when I saw him yesterday. His pants were dirty, he

   (iron) _____ _____ his shirt, and he *(shave)* _____ _____
   in several days.

7. Michael was very discouraged when I saw him last week. He had been on a diet for a month,

   and he *(lose)* _____ _____ any weight.

8. Sylvia fell several times while she was skiing last weekend. She *(ski)* _____

   _____ in a long time.

9. Arnold's boss fired him last week. Arnold *(get)* _____ _____ to work on time
   in six months.

10. Betty was very lucky she didn't miss her plane this morning. She got to the airport late, but

    the plane *(take off)* _____ _____ yet.

11. Alan did poorly on his English exam last week. I'm not surprised. He *(study)* _____

    _____ for the test.

12. Stuart enjoyed riding his bicycle last weekend. He *(ride)* _____ _____ it in a
    long time.

WORKING HARD

Jennifer was very busy after school yesterday.

1:00	write an English composition
2:00	study for my science test
3:00	practice the trombone
4:00	read the next history chapter
5:00	memorize my lines for the school play

What was she doing at 2:00?

1. _____ She was studying for her science test. _____

What had she already done?

2. _____ She had already written an English composition. _____

What hadn't she done yet?

3. _____ She hadn't practiced the trombone yet. _____

4. _____

5. _____

Brian had a very busy day at the office yesterday.

9:00	send an e-mail to the boss
10:00	give the employees their paychecks
11:00	hook up the new printer
1:00	write to the Bentley Company
2:00	take two packages to the post office

What was he doing at 11:00?

6. _____

What had he already done?

7. _____

8. _____

What hadn't he done yet?

9. _____

10. _____

Mr. and Mrs. Mendoza had a very busy day
at home yesterday.

8:00	assemble Billy's new bicycle
9:00	fix the fence
11:00	clean the garage
2:00	repair the roof
4:00	start to build a tree house

What were they doing at 11:00?

11. _____

What had they already done?

12. _____

13. _____

What hadn't they done yet?

14. _____

15. _____

Brenda wants to lose some weight, so she had
a very busy day at her health club.

9:00	do yoga
10:00	go jogging
12:00	play squash
3:00	lift weights
4:00	swim across the pool 10 times

What was she doing at 12:00?

16. _____

What had she already done?

17. _____

18. _____

What hadn't she done yet?

19. _____

20. _____

F WHAT HAD THEY BEEN DOING?

1. Professor Smith finally ended his lecture at 6:00. He *(talk)* _____ had been talking _____ for three hours.

2. The Millers moved out of their apartment building last week. They *(live)* _____ _____ there for several years.

3. Our daughter lost her job last week. She *(work)* _____ at the same company since she graduated from college.

4. Peter was happy when he and his girlfriend finally got married. They *(go out)* _____ _____ for eight years.

5. We were sad when Rudy's Restaurant closed. We *(plan)* _____ to eat there on our anniversary.

6. We felt very nostalgic when we went back to our hometown. We *(think about)* _____ _____ going back there for a long time.

7. My husband and I were happy when our son decided to study harder. He *(get)* _____ _____ poor grades in school.

8. Mr. Best was happy when his neighbor bought his own ladder. He *(borrow)* _____ _____ Mr. Best's ladder for many years.

9. I'm not surprised that Lenny's doctor put him on a diet. Lenny *(eat)* _____ too many fatty foods.

10. It's too bad your daughter wasn't able to perform in her violin recital last weekend. She *(rehearse)* _____ for it for a long time.

11. I'm sorry you had to cancel your trip to Hawaii. You and your wife *(look forward)* _____ _____ to it for a long time.

12. I'm so happy that Sally won the marathon last weekend. She *(train)* _____ for it for the past six months.

13. Nobody at the office was surprised when Mrs. Anderson fired Frank, her new assistant. He *(arrive)* _____ late for work every day for the past month.

G **GRAMMARRAP:** *George Had Been Thinking of Studying Greek*

Listen. Then clap and practice.

George had been thinking of studying Greek,

Moving to Athens and learning to speak.

But he changed his mind and decided to stay

With his family and friends and his dog in L.A.

Jill had been planning to learn how to ski,

But she tripped and fell and sprained her knee.

She had been dreaming of mountains and snow.

But now she's at home and has no place to go.

Marie had been planning to marry Tim,

But she fell in love with his brother, Jim.

Jim had been thinking of marrying Dee,

But everything changed when he met Marie.

H **LISTENING**

Listen to each word and then say it.

r!

1. reti<u>r</u>e
2. memo<u>r</u>ize
3. p<u>r</u>actice
4. d<u>r</u>ug sto<u>r</u>e
5. favo<u>r</u>ite
6. inte<u>rr</u>upt
7. a<u>r</u>ound
8. <u>r</u>estau<u>r</u>ant

9. live<u>l</u>y
10. loud<u>l</u>y
11. swo<u>ll</u>en
12. e<u>l</u>evator
13. f<u>l</u>y
14. be<u>l</u>ieve
15. co<u>l</u>d
16. fa<u>ll</u> as<u>l</u>eep

l!

I MARYLOU'S BROKEN KEYBOARD

Marylou's keyboard is broken. The r's and the l's don't always work. Fill in the missing r's and l's, and then read Marylou's letters aloud.

1.

_R_ oger,

I'm af _r_ aid the__e's something w__ong with the fi__ep__ace in the __iving __oom. A__so, the __ef__ige__ato__ is b__oken. I've been ca____ing the __and__o__d fo__ th__ee days on his ce____ phone, but he hasn't ca____ed back. I hope he ca____s me tomo____ow.

Ma__y__ou

2.

__ouise,

I'm te____ib__y wo____ied about my b__othe__ La____y's hea__th. He hu__t his __eg whi__e he was p__aying baseba____. He had a____eady dis__ocated his shou__der whi__e he was su__fing __ast F__iday. Acco__ding to his docto__, he is a__so having p__ob__ems with his b__ood p__essu__e and with his __ight w__ist. He __ea____y should t__y to __e__ax and take __ife a __itt__e easie__.

Ma__y__ou

3.

A__no__d,

Can you possib__y __ecommend a good __estau__ant in you__ neighbo__hood? I'm p__anning on taking my re__atives to __unch tomo____ow, but I'm not su__e whe__e.

We ate at a ve__y nice G__eek __estau__ant nea__ you__ apa__tment bui__ding __ast month, but I haven't been ab__e to __emembe__ the name. Do you know the p__ace?

You__ f__iend,
Ma__y__ou

4.

__osa,

I have been p__anning a t__ip to F__o__ida. I'____ be f__ying to O____ando on F__iday, and I'____ be __etu__ning th__ee days __ater. Have you eve__ been the__e? I __emembe__ you had fami__y membe__s who __ived in F__o__ida seve__a__ yea__s ago.

P__ease w__ite back.

A____ my __ove,
Ma__y__ou

Listen and choose the correct answer.

1. a. He can't find it anywhere.
    b. Where can it be?
    c. Nobody can hear him.

2. a. No, she isn't. She's my wife.
    b. Yes. She's my wife's cousin.
    c. No. She works for a different company.

3. a. Did you take a lot of photographs?
    b. Why did you charge it?
    c. That's too bad. You had been looking forward to it.

4. a. I know. He missed all his tests.
    b. I know. He's been doing very poorly.
    c. I know. He hasn't had a bad grade yet.

5. a. Did she find it?
    b. Whose is it?
    c. I'm sure it hurt a lot.

6. a. We stayed for the lecture.
    b. We talked about classical music.
    c. We read about psychology.

7. a. Did you enjoy yourselves?
    b. How many miles did you travel?
    c. Where did you drive?

8. a. She's having problems with her feet.
    b. She's having problems with her teeth.
    c. That's okay. We all make mistakes.

9. a. Did he make it?
    b. When did you get home?
    c. I know. He likes everything you serve.

10. a. You're right. I bought one.
    b. No, but I heard the noise.
    c. Sorry. We don't sell motorcycles.

11. a. I think so. He's been working hard.
    b. Yes. His plane will leave soon.
    c. I hope so. He never goes to work.

12. a. Poor Amy! She's always sick.
    b. Amy needs a new pair of boots.
    c. She was afraid to ask for it.

13. a. What a shame! Now she can't sing.
    b. What a shame! Now she can't knit.
    c. What a shame! Now she can't walk.

14. a. Would you like to talk about it?
    b. Who are you going to give it to?
    c. What did you decide to do?

15. a. I like you, too.
    b. What are you going to send me?
    c. You don't have anything to be jealous about.

16. a. Was it a very bad accident?
    b. Do you know anybody who can fix it?
    c. How long had they been going out?

17. a. I hope he feels better soon.
    b. What happened? Did you twist it?
    c. How are your cousins?

18. a. Did you call the doctor?
    b. What had you eaten?
    c. Why were you sad?

19. a. I'm glad to hear that.
    b. What was he angry about?
    c. What did he ask them?

20. a. We enjoyed the music.
    b. The lecture was very boring.
    c. The food was excellent.

21. a. They're too small.
    b. You have a job interview today.
    c. You have a baseball game today.

22. a. She enjoys going to the symphony.
    b. She enjoys going window-shopping.
    c. She enjoys doing gymnastics.

23. a. We're going to have a party.
    b. We're going on vacation.
    c. We received a lot of anniversary gifts.

24. a. He's glad he bought it.
    b. He's going to wear it for several years.
    c. He has to return it on Tuesday.

A. **Complete the sentences with the appropriate verb form.**

(eat) **1.** Why do you keep on _____ junk food?

(wrestle) **2.** My mother thinks _____ is dangerous.

(stop) **3.** I've decided _____ interrupting people all the time.

(box) **4.** Bruno practices _____ every day at the gym.

(swim) **5.** _____ is a good way to relax.

(skate) **6.** Where did your daughter learn _____ so well?

(talk) **7.** Please stop _____. I'm trying to sleep!

(do) **8.** Rita thinks that _____ exercises is a good way to start the day.

B. **Complete the sentences, using the past perfect tense.**

Ex. (wear) I wore my favorite striped tie to work yesterday. I ____hadn't worn____ it to work in a long time.

(start) By the time Andrew got to the play, it ___had___ already ___started___ .

(speak) **1.** I had dinner with some Japanese friends last night. I enjoyed myself very much

because I _____ Japanese in a long time.

(do) **2.** By the time Jennifer's father got home from work, she _____ already

_____ her homework, and she was ready to play baseball in the yard with him.

(leave) **3.** Ronald was upset. By the time he got to the train, it _____ already

_____ .

(write) **4.** I wrote an e-mail to my grandparents last night because I _____ to them for a few weeks.

(have) **5.** Patty had pizza for lunch yesterday. She _____ pizza in a long time.

(take) **6.** My husband and I took a walk after dinner last night. We _____ a walk after dinner in a long time.

(eat) **7.** I ate a big piece of chocolate cake last night and felt terrible about it. I _____

_____ a rich dessert since I started my diet.

(go) **8.** My parents went back to their hometown last month. They _____ back there for twenty years.

C. Complete the sentences, using the past perfect continuous tense.

Ex. (study)   Jonathan was glad he did well on his astronomy exam. He ____had been studying____ for it for days.

(work)   **1.** Marvin didn't get his promotion at work. He was heartbroken because he

_____ overtime for several months.

(train)   **2.** I was disappointed they canceled the marathon last week. I _____

_____ for it since last summer.

(argue)   **3.** Jane and John broke up last night. They _____ with each other for the past several weeks.

(plan)   **4.** Nancy caught a cold and couldn't go on her camping trip. It's a shame because she

_____ it since last April.

D. Listen and choose the correct answer.

Ex. (a.) go fishing.
    b. going canoeing.

1. a. tease her little brother.
    b. interrupting people.

2. a. moving to Miami.
    b. to sell our house.

3. a. to buy a sports car.
    b. buying a sports car.

4. a. waiting in line.
    b. drive downtown.

5. a. going out with Richard.
    b. ask for a raise.

WHAT ARE THEY SAYING?

1. A. Did you pick up Rover at the vet?

    B. No. I didn't _____pick him up_____.
        I thought YOU did.

2. A. Did you turn on the heat?

    B. Yes. I _____ a few
        hours ago, but it's still cold in here.

3. A. You should take back these library
        books.

    B. I know. I'll _____
        tomorrow morning.

4. A. Has Diane filled out her income tax
        forms?

    B. No. She's going to _____
        this weekend.

5. A. Where should we hang up this
        portrait?

    B. Let's _____
        over the fireplace.

6. A. I'm having trouble hooking up my
        computer.

    B. No problem. I'll _____.

7. A. Are you ever going to throw out these
        old souvenirs?

    B. I'll _____
        some day.

8. A. Did Sally take back her cell phone to
        the store?

    B. Yes. She _____
        this afternoon.

9. A. Did your daughter take down the
        photographs of her old boyfriend?

    B. Yes. She _____
        as soon as they stopped going out.

10. A. Did you remember to call up Aunt
        Clara to wish her "Happy Birthday"?

    B. Sorry. I didn't _____.
        I forgot it was her birthday.

| bring back | hand in | put away | put on | take off | turn off | turn on | wake up |

1. I think we should __turn on__ the air conditioner. It's getting very hot in here.

   Good idea. I'll _____ right away.

2. When are you going to __hand__ your biology report __in__?

   I'm going to _____ tomorrow morning. I have to write it tonight.

3. Let's _____ Mom and Dad! It's 8:00, and they're still sleeping!

   Don't _____. It's Saturday. They don't go to work today.

4. Don't forget to _____ the printer _____ before you leave the office tonight.

   You don't have to worry. I always _____ before I leave.

5. Why don't you _____ your hat and coat? It's warm in here.

   I'll _____ in a few minutes. I'm still a little cold.

6. Susie, when are you going to _____ your toys _____?

   I'm still playing with them. I'll _____ later.

7. Teddy, it's time for bed. _____ your pajamas _____!

   Okay, Dad. I'll _____ in a few minutes.

8. Do you think Richard will _____ his girlfriend _____ to the house after the dance?

   I don't know. Maybe he'll _____. I hope he does. I really want to meet her.

C GRAMMARRAP: *I Don't Know How!*

Listen. Then clap and practice.

A.   Take off your   skis.

Take them off   now!

B.   I can't take them   off.

I don't know   how!

A.   Turn off the   engine!

Turn it off   now!

B.   I can't turn it   off.

I don't know   how!

A.   Turn on the   oven!

Turn it on   now!

B.   I can't turn it   on.

I don't know   how!

A.   Hook up the   printer!

Hook it up   now!

B.   I can't hook it   up.

I don't know   how!

A.   Pick up the   suitcase.

Give it to   Jack.

B.   I can't pick it   up.

I have   a bad back!

A.   Take back   the videos!

Take them back today.

B.   I can't take them   back.

It's a holiday!

C **102**   **Activity Workbook**

cross out	give back	look up	throw away	turn off
do over	hook up	think over	turn down	write down

1. **Did your teacher like the composition you wrote about Australian birds?**

   No, she didn't. I have to _do it over_.

2. A. Do we still have the hammer we borrowed from our next-door neighbors?

   B. No, we don't. We _____ a long time ago.

3. A. What's the matter with the answering machine? Is it broken?

   B. No, it isn't. I forgot to _____.

4. A. Are you going to accept the invitation to Roger's wedding?

   B. I don't know. I have to _____ carefully. His wedding is in Alaska.

5. A. What's the weather forecast for tomorrow?

   B. I'm not sure. You should _____ on the Internet.

6. A. Is Kimberly going to the prom with Frank?

   B. No, she isn't. She had to _____ because she already had a date with somebody else.

7. A. What should I do with all these letters from my ex-boyfriend?

   B. I think you should _____.

8. A. What's Walter's new address?

   B. I can't remember. But I know I've _____ somewhere.

9. A. Should I erase all these mistakes in my math homework?

   B. No, I think you should just _____.

10. **Why aren't you watching the president's speech on TV?**

    I watched it for a while, but it was boring. So I

    _____.

James just moved into a new apartment. What does he have to do?

1. He has to ((put away)) / throw away his books and his clothes.

2. He has to fill out / hook up his printer and his computer

3. He has to take out / take back the moving truck he rented.

Jennifer is very happy and excited. She just got engaged. What's she going to do?

4. She's going to wake up / drop off her parents and tell them the news.

5. She's going to call off / call up all her friends.

6. She's going to look up / write down all the things her boyfriend said.

Mr. and Mrs. Baker's aunt and uncle are going to visit them next week. What do the Bakers have to do before then?

7. They have to clean up / take out their apartment.

8. They have to pick out / put away their children's toys.

9. They have to throw out / hook up all their old newspapers.

10. They have to call up / hang up their aunt and uncle's portrait.

F WHAT SHOULD THEY DO?

figure out	look up	throw out	use up
give back	think over	turn off	wake up

1. **Abigail, will you marry me?**   **That's a big decision, Howard. I have to _____think it over_____.**

2. A. I've been using my neighbor's screwdriver all summer.

   B. Don't you think it's time to _____?

3. A. Is there any more sugar?

   B. No. We _____. We have to buy some tomorrow.

4. A. I don't know the definition of this word.

   B. You really should _____ in the dictionary.

5. A. This math problem is very difficult.

   B. Maybe your mother can help you _____.

6. A. It's 7:30, and the children are still sleeping.

   B. They're going to be late for school. I'll _____.

7. A. It's really cold in here! Is the air conditioner on?

   B. Yes, it is. I'll _____ right away.

8. A. I'm very embarrassed. These are the worst photographs anyone has ever taken of me.

   B. Well, if they bother you that much, why don't you _____?

G LISTENING

Listen and choose the correct answer.

1. a. picked it up.
   b. used it up.

2. a. turn it down.
   b. turn it on.

3. a. take them down.
   b. turn them down.

4. a. think them over.
   b. drop them off.

5. a. hook it up.
   b. look it up.

6. a. give it back?
   b. hand it in?

7. a. throw it out.
   b. figure it out.

8. a. write it down.
   b. use it up.

9. a. pick it up.
   b. clean it up.

H COME UP WITH THE RIGHT ANSWER

call on	get over	look through	pick on	take after
get along with	hear from	look up to	run into	

1. I ____take after____ my father. We're both athletic, we're both interested in engineering, and we both like to paint. I'm really

glad I ____take after him____.

2. I haven't _____ my son in three weeks. He's

at college, and I usually _____ every week!

3. I'm so embarrassed. My teacher _____ me twice in class today, but I didn't know ANY of the answers. I have to study

tonight. She might _____ again tomorrow.

4. My husband and I enjoyed _____ our wedding

pictures. We hadn't _____ in years.

5. Jack _____ his cold very quickly. I think he

_____ fast because he stayed home and took care of himself.

6. I really _____ my grandmother. She's honest, she's intelligent, and she's very generous. I hope someday when I'm a

grandmother, my grandchildren will _____, too.

7. I was very surprised. I _____ my old girlfriend at the

bank yesterday morning. And then I _____ again at a movie last night.

8. I don't _____ my mother-in-law. We often

disagree. All the people in our family _____. Why can't I?

9. Bobby is mean. He _____ his cats all the time.

The cats don't like it when Bobby _____.

106   Activity Workbook

Listen. Then clap and practice.

I don't   get along with   Kate and   Clem.

I almost   never   hear from   them.

But I get along   well   with Bob   and Fay.

I call them   up   three times   a day.

Jack   takes after   his Uncle   Jim.

Bob   looks up to   his father,   Tim.

Kate never   picks on   her sister,   Sue.

But she always   picks on   her brother,   Lou.

J **CHOOSE**

1. A. Do we have any more pens?
   B. No, we don't. We _____.
   a. ran into them
   b. ran out of them *(circled)*

2. A. Does Carol still have the flu?
   B. No. She _____ a few days ago.
   a. got over it
   b. got it over

3. A. Does Jill get along with her brother?
   B. No. He _____ all the time.
   a. picks her on
   b. picks on her

4. A. I can't remember Tom's phone number.
   B. You should _____.
   a. look up to him
   b. look it up

5. A. Amy knows all the answers in class.
   B. Does the teacher always _____?
   a. call on her
   b. call her on

6. A. This is a very difficult problem.
   B. I know. I can't _____.
   a. figure out it
   b. figure it out

7. A. Have you heard from Pam recently?
   B. Yes. I _____ the other day.
   a. heard her from
   b. heard from her

8. A. What should I do with these old letters?
   B. Why don't you _____?
   a. throw them out
   b. throw out them

9. A. These photographs are wonderful!
   B. I know. Let's _____ again.
   a. look through them
   b. look them through

10. A. Do you like William?
    B. Oh, yes. I _____ very well.
    a. get him along
    b. get along with him

11. A. Should I turn off the computer?
    B. No. You can _____.
    a. leave it on
    b. leave on it

12. A. Did you hang up your uncle's portrait?
    B. No, I didn't. I _____.
    a. took it down
    b. took down it

13. A. You look like your father.
    B. I know. Everybody says I _____.
    a. take him after
    b. take after him

14. A. They have a very unusual last name.
    B. You'll remember it if you _____.
    a. write down it
    b. write it down

K WHAT DOES IT MEAN?

Choose the correct answer.

1. Richard takes after his mother.
   a. He's always with her.
   b. They're both shy. *(circled)*
   c. His mother always arrives first.

2. Please turn off the air conditioner.
   a. It's too hot in this room.
   b. The room is too small.
   c. It's too cold in this room.

3. Tom left his briefcase on the plane.
   a. Maybe his mind slipped.
   b. He forgot it.
   c. He was very careful.

4. I'm going to take these pants back.
   a. They're new.
   b. They're medium.
   c. They're too baggy.

5. Fran can't find her notebook.
   a. I hope she didn't throw it out.
   b. I hope she didn't fill it out.
   c. I hope she didn't take it off.

6. Bob doesn't get along with his neighbors.
   a. He can't stand to talk to them.
   b. He likes them very much.
   c. He looks up to them.

7. I hope I don't run into my old boyfriend.
   a. Why? Will he get hurt?
   b. Why don't you want to see him?
   c. Why? Does he like to jog?

8. Paul had to do his homework over.
   a. It was excellent.
   b. He didn't think it over.
   c. He had made a lot of mistakes.

L LISTENING

Listen and choose the correct answer.

1. a. He's very tall.
   b. I can never find him.
   c. I want to be like him. *(circled)*

2. a. You're lucky he has a car.
   b. I'm sure that bothers you.
   c. Do you also pick him up?

3. a. Yes. I put it in the closet.
   b. Yes. I gave it to our neighbor.
   c. Yes. We had used it all up.

4. a. I'm sorry you're still sick.
   b. I'm glad you're feeling better.
   c. It's too bad you have to do it over.

5. a. No. He speaks very softly.
   b. Yes. He sent me an e-mail yesterday.
   c. No. I haven't heard him recently.

6. a. The music was very loud.
   b. Somebody had picked it up.
   c. I already had another date.

7. a. Yes, several times.
   b. Yes, but I wasn't home.
   c. Yes, but I had already left the house.

8. a. He didn't need it anymore.
   b. It was already at the cleaner's.
   c. I know. He found one he really liked.

9. a. Did she hurt herself?
   b. How did you hurt yourself?
   c. When does her plane leave?

10. a. The store isn't having a sale.
    b. Everything in the store is cheaper.
    c. Everything is 20 cents less this week.

11. a. Good. I'll buy it.
    b. Don't worry. We have larger ones.
    c. I know. It's too tight.

12. a. Yes. I used up four pair.
    b. Yes. I put on four pair.
    c. Yes. I looked up four pair.

1.

I ate too much.   So ___did I___.

2.

I hate to go to the mall.   _____, too.

3.

I can play the trombone.   So _____.

4.

I'm allergic to milk.   _____, too.

5.

I'll be starting college this fall.   _____, too.

6.

I was late for work.   So _____.

7.

I'm going to retire soon.   So _____.

8.

I've been doing poorly in school recently.   _____, too.

9.

I just got a promotion.   _____, too.

10.

I'll be on vacation next week.   So _____.

11.

I have to lose a little weight.   So _____.

A. Do you live near here?

B. Yes. I live on Center Street.

A. Really? So ___*do I*___ ¹. I live in the new apartment building at the corner of Center Street and Broadway.

B. What a coincidence! _____ ², too. I guess we're neighbors. My name is Frank Winters.

A. Hi. I'm Steve Green. Nice to meet you.

B. Nice meeting you, too. So how long have you been living there?

A. I moved in last week.

B. What a coincidence! _____ ³, too. I've been very busy since I got here.

A. So _____ ⁴. Moving into a new apartment isn't easy.

B. You're right. It isn't. Tell me, have you found a job yet?

A. Yes, I have. I'll be working at Mason's Department Store.

B. I don't believe it! _____ ⁵, too.

A. What department will you be working in?

B. I got a job in the Men's Clothing Department.

A. What a coincidence! So _____ ⁶. I was a salesperson in my last job also.

B. _____ ⁷, too. I sold men's clothing.

A. I can't believe it! _____ ⁸, too.

B. I'm on my way to work right now.

A. _____ ⁹, too. Do you want to have lunch together?

B. Sure. I have a lunch break at noon.

A. So _____ ¹⁰. Let's meet for lunch in the company cafeteria.

B. Okay. That'll be nice. I'm looking forward to it.

A. So _____ ¹¹.

1. I didn't like the movie.
   Neither ___did I___ .

2. I'm not feeling very well.
   _____ either.

3. I wasn't in school yesterday.
   Neither _____.

4. I can't play tennis very well.
   _____ either.

5. I won't be home tonight.
   _____ either.

6. I've never been in the hospital before.
   Neither _____.

7. I can't stand driving in traffic.
   _____ either.

8. I'm not going to order dessert.
   Neither _____.

9. I didn't enjoy the lecture.
   _____ either.

10. I don't like to practice the piano.
    Neither _____.

11. I'll never go sailing again.
    Neither _____.

Listen and complete the sentences.

1. So _____did I_____.

2. _____, too.

3. So _____.

4. _____ either.

5. _____, too.

6. _____, too.

7. Neither _____.

8. _____, too.

9. Neither _____.

10. So _____.

11. _____ either.

12. _____, too.

13. Neither _____.

14. So _____.

15. _____ either.

E **GRAMMARRAP:** *So Do I*

Listen. Then clap and practice.

A. I like to   fly.

B. So do   I.

A. They like to   ski.

B. So do   we.

A. She likes the   zoo.

B. He does,   too.

A. You're a good   friend.

B. So are   you.

F **GRAMMARRAP:** *They Didn't Either*

Listen. Then clap and practice.

We didn't   eat it.

They didn't   either.

He didn't   finish it.

Neither did   she.

She wasn't   hungry.

He wasn't   either.

They weren't   hungry.

Neither were   we.

1. Why were you and your brother late for school today?

   I had to go to the dentist, and so ____did he____.

2. Will you and your wife be home this evening?

   I don't think so. I'll be working late, and so _____.

3. How did you and Tom feel after you ran in the marathon?

   I was exhausted, and _____, too.

4. Would you and your sister like to learn how to ski?

   Actually, I've already tried it, and so _____.

5. Can Ricky and I go to the movies tonight?

   He should study for his English exam, and _____, too.

6. Have you seen Mr. and Mrs. Martinez recently?

   I saw them today. I was in the park, and _____, too.

7. Should I go into the water with Timmy and Susie?

   No. That's okay. Timmy can swim, and _____ Susie.

8. Why weren't you and your brother at baseball practice today?

   I had to help my mother, and so _____.

9. Why are you and your wife leaving the party?

   She has to get up early tomorrow, and _____, too.

10. Why are your parents so worried?

    I've decided to ....
    ....,
    and _____ my brother.

1. Are you and your brother going to be in the school play?

Unfortunately, he can't act, and neither _____can I_____ .

2. Why do you and your friends look so upset?

I didn't do very well on the math test, and _____ either.

3. Did you and your son see the baseball game on TV today?

No, we didn't. I'm not interested in sports, and neither _____ .

4. Are you and your sister going to go to the concert tonight?

No, we aren't. I don't like folk music, and _____ either.

5. Why did you and your friends leave the dance so early last night?

I wasn't having a very good time, and neither _____ .

6. Have you and your wife made plans for your vacation yet?

I haven't had very much time, and _____ either.

7. Are you and your roommates going to Sally's wedding?

No, we aren't. I won't be here this weekend, and neither _____ .

8. It's getting late. Should I make dinner now?

The truth is, I'm not very hungry, and the children _____ .

9. Is the DVD player still broken?

Yes, it is. I haven't been able to fix it, and _____ your father.

10. How was your date with Samantha last night?

We were both a little nervous. I had never gone out on a date before, and _____ either.

so	too	either	neither

1. A. Why didn't Ronald and his wife go to work yesterday?

   B. He had a terrible cold,

   and { _____*so did she*_____.

   { _____*she did, too*_____.

2. A. Did Betty and Bob enjoy the concert last night?

   B. Not really. She couldn't hear the music,

   and { _____.

   { _____.

3. A. Do Jack and his girlfriend enjoy going sailing?

   B. No, they don't. She gets seasick,

   and { _____.

   { _____.

4. A. Why didn't Mr. and Mrs. Miller order the cheesecake for dessert?

   B. He doesn't eat rich foods,

   and { _____.

   { _____.

5. A. Why did Beverly and Brian have trouble doing their chemistry experiments?

   B. He hadn't followed the instructions,

   and { _____.

   { _____.

6. A. Why aren't you and Peter good friends any more?

   B. I'm in love with Amanda Richardson,

   and { _____.

   { _____.

1. I'm tall, but my sister and brother _____aren't_____. I've always _____ the tallest person in our family.

2. My brother isn't very athletic, but my sister _____. She enjoys _____ squash and _____ gymnastics.

3. I can't draw pictures, but my brother _____. He's been _____ pictures since he _____ four years old.

4. My brother and I have different interests. I enjoy seeing movies, but my brother _____. He enjoys _____ to lectures and concerts.

5. My mother is interested in photography, but my father _____. My mother _____ photographs since she was a teenager.

6. My father has lived here all his life, but his parents _____. They've _____ in this country _____ fifty years. Before that, they _____ in Italy.

7. My grandparents sometimes speak to us in Italian, but my father _____. He _____ Italian to anyone in a long time.

8. I'll be going to college next year, but my brother _____. He _____ finished high school yet.

9. I don't have a very good voice, but my sister _____. She sings in the school choir. She has _____ in the choir _____ she started high school.

10. I'm usually very neat, but my sister and brother _____. They never hang _____ their clothes or put _____ their books.

11. I know how to ski, but my brother _____. I've been skiing _____ the past nine years.

12. My sister is a very good skater, but my brother and I _____. We just started _____ a month ago. Before that, we _____ never _____ at all.

K LISTENING

Listen and complete the sentences.

1. but my husband _____didn't_____.

2. but my daughter _____.

3. but you _____.

4. but I _____.

5. but my friends _____.

6. but my wife _____.

7. but you _____.

8. but my brother _____.

9. but everybody else _____.

10. but our teacher _____.

11. but my son _____.

12. but the other man _____.

13. but my sister _____.

14. but I _____.

15. but my friends _____.

16. but my brother _____.

17. but my children _____.

18. but I _____.

L GRAMMARRAP: *I've Been Working Hard, and You Have, Too*

Listen. Then clap and practice.

I've been working hard, and   you have,   too.

I'm   exhausted,   and so   are you.

He's been   out of town,   and so   has she.

They've been very   busy,   and so   have we.

I   didn't go,   and neither   did he.

They   weren't there,   and neither   were we.

We   stayed home,   and so   did they.

Nobody   went   to the meeting   that day.

I don't speak   Greek,   but my brother   does.

I wasn't born in   Greece,   but my mother   was.

I didn't study   Greek,   but my brother   did.

He's spoken   Greek   since he was   a kid.

Activity Workbook   117

M SOUND IT OUT!

Listen to each word and then say it.

f<u>u</u>ll		f<u>oo</u>l	
1. l<u>oo</u>k	**3.** p<u>u</u>t	**1.** n<u>oo</u>n	**3.** J<u>u</u>dy
2. c<u>ou</u>ld	**4.** f<u>oo</u>t	**2.** dr<u>ew</u>	**4.** f<u>oo</u>d

Listen and put a circle around the word that has the same sound.

1. f<u>u</u>ll:	p<u>oo</u>l	(c<u>oo</u>ks)	sh<u>oe</u>
2. fl<u>u</u>:	t<u>oo</u>	w<u>ou</u>ld	bl<u>oo</u>d
3. g<u>oo</u>d:	s<u>ou</u>p	sh<u>ou</u>ldn't	J<u>u</u>ne
4. w<u>oo</u>d:	fl<u>u</u>	t<u>oo</u>th	p<u>u</u>t
5. c<u>ou</u>ld:	c<u>u</u>p	c<u>oo</u>kies	<u>u</u>pstairs
6. h<u>oo</u>k:	f<u>oo</u>d	m<u>o</u>vie	g<u>oo</u>d
7. w<u>o</u>man:	s<u>u</u>gar	tr<u>ue</u>	n<u>ew</u>

Now make a sentence using all the words you circled, and read the sentence aloud.

8. .... much ....

in their ....

9. s<u>ui</u>t:	tw<u>o</u>	p<u>u</u>t	b<u>u</u>s
10. c<u>oo</u>k:	f<u>oo</u>d	b<u>oo</u>ks	s<u>u</u>nny
11. f<u>oo</u>t:	b<u>oo</u>kcase	p<u>oo</u>l	m<u>u</u>st
12. bl<u>ue</u>:	j<u>u</u>st	wh<u>o</u>	l<u>oo</u>ked
13. w<u>ou</u>ld:	s<u>ui</u>t	t<u>oo</u>l	t<u>oo</u>k
14. c<u>oo</u>l:	st<u>oo</u>d	aftern<u>oo</u>n	p<u>u</u>lse
15. sch<u>oo</u>l:	S<u>u</u>san's	th<u>u</u>nder	fl<u>oo</u>r

Now make a sentence using all the words you circled, and read the sentence aloud.

16. .... from ....

.... this .... ?

_____j_____ 1. afford

_____ 2. argue

_____ 3. bachelor

_____ 4. begin

_____ 5. bump into

_____ 6. can't stand

_____ 7. compatible

_____ 8. consider

_____ 9. continue

_____ 10. discuss

_____ 11. exam

_____ 12. exhausted

_____ 13. fail

_____ 14. frightened

_____ 15. hike

_____ 16. injure

_____ 17. lately

_____ 18. outgoing

_____ 19. prepared

_____ 20. price

_____ 21. return

_____ 22. review

_____ 23. stand in line

_____ 24. teach

_____ 25. use up

_____ 26. vegetarian

a. afraid

b. do poorly

c. fight

d. finish

e. friendly and talkative

f. give back

g. give lessons

h. hate

i. have a lot in common

j. have enough money

k. how much it costs

l. hurt

m. keep on

n. meet

o. ready

p. recently

q. single man

r. someone who doesn't eat meat

s. start

t. study again

u. take a long walk

v. talk about

w. test

x. think about

y. tired

z. wait

✓ CHECK-UP TEST: Chapters 9-10

A. Complete the sentences.

Ex. My son is waiting for me at the bus stop. I have to pick ___him___ ___up___ right away.

My mother and I are both tall with curly hair. Everybody says I take ___after___ ___her___.

1. I'll finish my homework in a little while, and then I'll hand _____ _____.

2. My father is a very smart man. I really look _____ _____ _____.

3. I haven't talked to Aunt Shirley lately. I hope I hear _____ _____ soon.

4. My English teacher didn't like my composition. I have to do _____ _____.

5. I don't know the definition of this word. I need to look _____ _____.

6. I can't find any flour. I think we ran _____ _____ _____.

7. I can't find my wallet. Could you help me look _____ _____?

8. Don't leave your clothes on the bed. You really should hang _____ _____.

9. Don't worry about your mistakes. You can always cross _____ _____.

10. I can never remember Alan's address. I should write _____ _____.

11. I've had the flu for the past several days. My doctor says I'll get _____ _____ soon.

B. Complete the sentences.

so	too	neither	either

Ex. Maria did well on her science test, and _____so did_____ her sister.

1. I'm wearing new shoes today, and _____ my brother.

2. I won't be able to come to the meeting tomorrow, and _____ Barbara.

3. I was bored during Professor Gray's lecture, and my friends _____.

4. Janet can't skate, and her brother _____.

5. I've been taking guitar lessons for years, and _____ my sisters.

6. David worked overtime yesterday, and his wife _____.

7. Louise has never been to Europe, and _____ her husband.

8. I want to complain to the landlord, and _____ my neighbors.

9. I'm not very athletic, and _____ my wife.

C. Listen and complete the sentences.

Ex. but her husband _____*doesn't*_____ .

1. but my sister _____ .

2. but my parents _____ .

3. but my brother _____ .

4. but my wife _____ .

5. but I _____ .

Listening Scripts

Page 7 Exercise H
Listen to each question and then complete the answer.

1. Does Jim like to play soccer?
2. Is Alice working today?
3. Are those students staying after school today?
4. Do Mr. and Mrs. Jackson work hard?
5. Does your wife still write poetry?
6. Is it raining?
7. Is he busy?
8. Do you have to leave?
9. Does your sister play the violin?
10. Is your brother studying in the library?
11. Are you wearing a necklace today?
12. Do you and your husband go camping very often?
13. Is your niece doing her homework?
14. Are they still chatting online?
15. Do you and your friends play Scrabble very often?

Page 13 Exercise B
Listen and circle the correct answer.

1. They work.
2. They worked.
3. We study English.
4. I waited for the bus.
5. We visit our friends.
6. She met important people.
7. He taught Chinese.
8. She delivers the mail.
9. I wrote letters to my friends.
10. I ride my bicycle to work.
11. He sleeps very well.
12. I had a terrible headache.

Page 26 Exercise C
Listen and choose the time of the action.

1. My daughter is going to sing Broadway show tunes in her high school show.
2. Janet bought a new dress for her friend's party.
3. Are you going to go out with George?
4. I went shopping at the new mall.
5. How did you poke yourself in the eye?
6. Who's going to prepare dinner?
7. Did the baby sleep well?
8. I'm really looking forward to Saturday night.
9. Is your son going to play games on his computer?
10. We're going to complain to the landlord about the heat in our apartment.
11. We bought a dozen donuts.
12. I'm going to take astronomy.

Page 33 Exercise L
Listen to each story. Then answer the questions.

What Are Mr. and Mrs. Miller Looking Forward to?

Mr. and Mrs. Miller moved into their new house in Los Angeles last week. They're happy because the house has a large, bright living room and a big, beautiful yard. They're looking forward to life in their new home. Every weekend they'll be able to relax in their living room and enjoy the beautiful California weather in their big, beautiful yard. But this weekend Mr. and Mrs. Miller won't be relaxing. They're going to be very busy. First, they're going to repaint the living room. Then, they're going to assemble their new computer and VCR. And finally, they're going to plant some flowers in their yard. They'll finally be able to relax NEXT weekend.

What's Jonathan Looking Forward to?

I'm so excited! I'm sitting at my computer in my office, but I'm not thinking about my work today. I'm thinking about next weekend because next Saturday is the day I'll be getting married. After the wedding, my wife and I will be going to Hawaii for a week. I can't wait! For one week, we won't be working, we won't be cooking, we won't be cleaning, and we won't be paying bills. We'll be swimming in the ocean, relaxing on the beach, and eating in fantastic restaurants.

What's Mrs. Grant Looking Forward to?

Mrs. Grant is going to retire this year, and she's really looking forward to her new life. She won't be getting up early every morning and taking the bus to work. She'll be able to sleep late every day of the week. She'll read books, she'll work in her garden, and she'll go to museums with her friends. And she's very happy that she'll be able to spend more time with her grandchildren. She'll take them to the park to feed the birds, she'll take them to the zoo to see the animals, and she'll baby-sit when her son and daughter-in-law go out on Saturday nights.

Page 35 Exercise E
Listen to each question and then complete the answer.

Ex. Does your brother like to swim?
1. Are you going to buy donuts tomorrow?
2. Will Jennifer and John see each other again soon?
3. Doctor, did I sprain my ankle?
4. Does Tommy have a black eye?
5. Is your daughter practicing the violin?
6. Do you and your husband go to the movies very often?
7. Does Diane go out with her boyfriend every Saturday evening?
8. Will you and your wife be visiting us tonight?

Page 36 Exercise B
Listen and choose the word you hear.

1. I've ridden them for many years.
2. Yes. I've taken French.
3. I'm giving injections.
4. I've driven one for many years.
5. Yes. I've written it.
6. I'm drawing it right now.
7. I've spoken it for many years.
8. Yes. I've drawn that.

Page 37 Exercise D
Is Speaker B answering Yes or No? Listen to each conversation and circle the correct answer.

1. A. Do you know how to drive a bus?
   B. I've driven a bus for many years.

2. A. I usually take the train to work. Do you also take the train?
   B. Actually, I've never taken the train to work.

3. A. Are you a good swimmer?
   B. To tell the truth, I've never swum very well.

4. A. Did you get up early this morning?
   B. I've gotten up early every morning this week.

5. A. I'm going to give my dog a bath today. Do you have any advice?
   B. Sorry. I don't. I've never given my dog a bath.

6. A. Do you like to eat sushi?
   B. Of course! I've eaten sushi for many years.

7. A. I just got a big raise! Did you also get one?
   B. Actually, I've never gotten a raise.

8. A. I did very well on the math exam. How about you?
   B. I've never done well on a math exam.

Page 47 Exercise O

What things have these people done? What haven't they done? Listen and check Yes *or* No.

1. A. Carla, have you done your homework yet?
   B. Yes, I have. I did my homework this morning.
   A. And have you practiced the violin?
   B. No, I haven't practiced yet. I promise I'll practice this afternoon.

2. A. Kevin?
   B. Yes, Mrs. Blackwell?
   A. Have you written your report yet?
   B. No, I haven't. I'll write it immediately.
   A. And have you sent a fax to the Crane Company?
   B. No, I haven't. I promise I'll send them a fax after I write the report.

3. A. Have you fed the dog yet?
   B. Yes, I have. I fed him a few minutes ago.
   A. Good. Well, I guess we can leave for work now.
   B. But we haven't eaten breakfast yet!

4. A. I'm leaving now, Mr. Green.
   B. Have you fixed the pipes in the basement, Charlie?
   A. Yes, I have.
   B. And have you repaired the washing machine?
   A. Yes, I have. It's working again.
   B. That's great! Thank you, Charlie.
   A. I'll send you a bill, Mr. Green.

5. A. You know, we haven't done the laundry all week.
   B. I know. We should do it today.
   A. We also haven't vacuumed the rugs!
   B. We haven't?
   A. No, we haven't.
   B. Oh. I guess we should vacuum them today.

6. A. Are we ready for the party?
   B. I think so. We've gotten all the food at the supermarket, and we've cleaned the house from top to bottom!
   A. Well, I guess we're ready for the party!

7. A. Have you spoken to the landlord about our broken light?
   B. Yes, I have. I spoke to him this morning.
   A. What did he say?
   B. He said we should call an electrician.
   A. Okay. Let's call Ajax Electric.
   B. Don't worry. I've already called them, and they're coming this afternoon.

8. A. Have you hooked up the new VCR yet?
   B. I can't do it. It's really difficult.
   A. Have you read the instructions?
   B. Yes, I have. I've read them ten times, and I still can't understand them!

Page 56 Exercise E

Listen and choose the correct answer.

1. Bob has been engaged since he got out of the army.
2. My sister Carol has been a professional musician since she finished music school.
3. Michael has been home since he fell and hurt himself last week.
4. My wife has gotten up early every morning since she started her new job.
5. Richard has eaten breakfast in the school cafeteria every morning since he started college.
6. Nancy and Tom have known each other for five and a half years.
7. My friend Charlie and I have played soccer every weekend since we were eight years old.
8. Patty has had short hair since she was a teenager.
9. Ron has owned his own business since he moved to Chicago nine years ago.
10. I've been interested in astronomy for the past eleven years.
11. I use my personal computer all the time. I've had it since I was in high school.
12. Alan has had problems with his house since he bought it fifteen years ago.

Page 61 Exercise L

Listen and choose the correct answer.

1. A. Have you always been a salesperson?
   B. No. I've been a salesperson for the past four years. Before that, I was a cashier.

2. A. How long has your daughter been in medical school?
   B. She's been in medical school for the past two years.

3. A. Have your parents always lived in a house?
   B. No. They've lived in a house for the past ten years. Before that, they lived in an apartment.

4. A. How long have you wanted to be an actor?
   B. I've wanted to be an actor since I was in college. Before that, I wanted to be a musician.

5. A. Do you and your husband still exercise at your health club every day?
   B. No. We haven't done that for a year.

6. A. Has James been a bachelor all his life?
   B. No, he hasn't. He was married for ten years.

7. A. Has your sister Jane always wanted to be a writer?
   B. Yes, she has. She's wanted to be a writer all her life.

8. A. Have you ever broken your ankle?
   B. No. I've sprained it a few times, but I've never broken it.

9. A. Have you always liked classical music?
   B. No. I've liked classical music for the past few years. Before that, I liked rock music.

10. A. Has Billy had a sore throat for a long time?
    B. He's had a sore throat for the past two days. Before that, he had a fever.

11. A. Jennifer has been the store manager since last fall.
    B. What did she do before that?
    A. She was a salesperson.

12. A. Have you always been interested in modern art?
    B. No. I've been interested in modern art since I moved to Paris a few years ago. Before that, I was only interested in sports.

Page 64 Exercise E

Listen and choose the correct time expressions to complete the sentences.

1. A. How long have you been living there?
   B. I've been living there since . . .
2. A. How long has your daughter been practicing the piano?
   B. She's been practicing for . . .
3. A. How long have I been running?
   B. You've been running since . . .
4. A. How long have you been feeling bad?
   B. I've been feeling bad for . . .
5. A. How long have they been waiting?
   B. They've been waiting for . . .
6. A. How long has your son been studying?
   B. He's been studying since . . .
7. A. How long have your sister and her boyfriend been dating?
   B. They've been dating since . . .
8. A. Dad, how long have we been driving?
   B. Hmm. I think we've been driving for . . .
9. A. How long has your little girl been crying?
   B. She's been crying for . . .

Page 67 Exercise H

Listen and choose what the people are talking about.

1. She's been directing it for an hour.
2. We've been rearranging it all morning.
3. I've been paying them on time.
4. He's been playing them for years.
5. Have you been bathing them for a long time?
6. They've been rebuilding it for a year.
7. She's been writing it for a week.
8. He's been translating them for many years.
9. I've been reading it all afternoon.
10. She's been knitting them for a few weeks.
11. We've been listening to them all afternoon.
12. I've been recommending it for years.
13. They've been repairing it all day.
14. She's been taking it all morning.
15. I've been solving them all my life.

Page 71 Exercise L

Listen and decide where the conversation is taking place.

1. A. I'm really tired.
   B. No wonder! You've been chopping tomatoes for the past hour.
2. A. Mark! I'm surprised. You've been falling asleep in class all morning, and you've never fallen asleep in class before.
   B. I'm sorry, Mrs. Applebee. It won't happen again.
3. A. I've been washing these shirts for the past half hour, and they still aren't clean.
   B. Here. Try this Presto Soap.
4. A. We've been standing in line for an hour and forty-five minutes.
   B. I know. I hope the movie is good. I've never stood in line for such a long time.

5. A. What seems to be the problem, Mr. Jones?
   B. My back has been hurting me for the past few days.
   A. I'm sorry to hear that.
6. A. You know, we've been reading here for more than two hours.
   B. You're right. I think it's time to go now.
7. A. Do you want to leave?
   B. I think so. We've seen all the paintings here.
8. A. How long have you been exercising?
   B. For an hour and a half.
9. A. We've been waiting for an hour, and it still isn't here.
   B. I know. I'm going to be late for work.
10. A. I think we've seen them all. Which one do you want to buy?
    B. I like that black one over there.
11. A. We've been watching this movie for the past hour, and it's terrible!
    B. You're right. Let's change the channel.
12. A. I've got a terrible headache.
    B. Why?
    A. Customers have been complaining all morning.
    B. What have they been complaining about?
    A. Some people have been complaining about our terrible products, but most people have been complaining about our high prices.

Page 77 Exercise F

Listen and choose the correct answer.

1. A. How long has Janet been an actress?
   B. She's been an actress since she graduated from acting school.
2. A. Have you watched the news yet?
   B. Yes. I saw the president, and I heard his speech.
3. A. Have you always lived in Denver?
   B. No. We've lived in Denver since 1995. Before that, we lived in New York.
4. A. Has Dad made dinner yet?
   B. Not yet. He still has to make it.
5. A. How long has your ceiling been leaking?
   B. It's been leaking for more than a week.
   A. Have you called the superintendent?
   B. Yes, I have. I've called him several times.
6. A. Billy is having trouble with his homework.
   B. Has he asked anyone to help him?
   A. No, he hasn't.

Page 87 Exercise N

Listen and choose the correct answer.

1. Dr. Gomez really enjoys . . .
2. Whenever possible, my wife and I try to avoid . . .
3. Next summer I'm going to learn . . .
4. Every day Rita practices . . .
5. My parents have decided . . .
6. I've considered . . .
7. Are you thinking about . . .
8. I'm going to quit . . .
9. Why do you keep on . . .
10. My doctor says I should stop . . .
11. David can't stand . . .
12. Are you going to continue to . . .

13. James doesn't want to start . . .
14. Next semester Kathy is going to begin . . .
15. You know, you can't keep on . . .

Page 97 Exercise J
Listen and choose the correct answer.

1. Steve lost his voice.
2. Is Beverly one of your relatives?
3. We just canceled our trip to South America.
4. Ricky has been failing all of his tests this year.
5. Francine dislocated her shoulder.
6. What did you and your students discuss in class?
7. My girlfriend and I rode on the roller coaster yesterday.
8. Grandma can't chew this piece of steak very well.
9. Jimmy loves my homemade food.
10. Did you see the motorcycles go by?
11. Do you think Mr. Montero will take a day off soon?
12. Amy wanted to ask her boss for a raise, but she got cold feet.
13. Have you heard that Margaret sprained her wrist?
14. I have to make an important decision.
15. I envy you.
16. I feel terrible. Debbie and Dan broke up last week.
17. My ankle hurts a lot.
18. I was heartbroken when I heard what happened.
19. Michael was furious with his neighbors.
20. We went to a recital last night.
21. Tom, don't forget to shine your shoes!
22. My friend Carla is extremely athletic.
23. My husband and I have been writing invitations all afternoon.
24. Charles rented a beautiful tuxedo for his niece's wedding.

Page 99 Exercise D
Listen and choose the correct answer.

Ex. My grandfather likes to . . .
1. Susan says she's going to stop . . .
2. My wife and I are thinking about . . .
3. David is considering . . .
4. I can't stand to . . .
5. You should definitely keep on . . .

Page 105 Exercise G
Listen and choose the correct answer.

1. A. I looked in the refrigerator, and I can't find the orange juice.
   B. That's because we . . .
2. A. I'm frustrated! My computer isn't working today.
   B. I think you forgot to . . .
3. A. What should I do with the Christmas decorations?
   B. I think it's time to . . .
4. A. Should I take these clothes to the cleaner's?
   B. Yes. You should definitely . . .
5. A. Hmm. What does this word mean?
   B. You should . . .
6. A. I have to return this skateboard to my cousin.
   B. When are you going to . . . ?
7. A. This math problem is very difficult.
   B. Maybe I can . . .
8. A. I'll never remember their new telephone number.
   B. You should . . .
9. A. I just spilled milk on the kitchen floor!
   B. Don't worry. I'll . . .

Page 108 Exercise L
Listen and choose the correct answer.

1. I really look up to my father.
2. My brother picks on me all the time.
3. Did you throw away the last can of paint?
4. I still haven't gotten over the flu.
5. Have you heard from your cousin Sam recently?
6. Why did you turn him down?
7. Did your French teacher call on you today?
8. George picked out a new suit for his wedding.
9. I have to drop my sister off at the airport.
10. Everything in the store is 20 percent off this week.
11. This jacket fits you.
12. Did you try on a lot of shoes?

Page 112 Exercise D
Listen and complete the sentences.

1. I missed the bus this morning.
2. I'm allergic to nuts.
3. I'll be on vacation next week.
4. I've never flown in a helicopter.
5. I can speak Chinese.
6. I like to go sailing.
7. I'm not going to the company picnic this weekend.
8. I saw a very good movie last night.
9. I don't go on many business trips.
10. I've been to London several times.
11. I'm not a vegetarian.
12. I should lose a little weight.
13. I can't stop worrying about my health.
14. I hate to drive downtown.
15. I won't be able to go to Nancy's party this Saturday night.

Page 117 Exercise K
Listen and complete the sentences.

1. I missed the bus today, . . .
2. I'm allergic to cats, . . .
3. I'll be on vacation next week, . . .
4. You've never seen a rainbow, . . .
5. I can speak Italian, . . .
6. I like to go sailing, . . .
7. I've been on television several times, . . .
8. I saw an exciting movie last weekend, . . .
9. I won't be in the office tomorrow, . . .
10. We were late, . . .
11. I'm not a vegetarian, . . .
12. I saw the stop sign, . . .
13. I can't swim very well, . . .
14. They have to work overtime this weekend, . . .
15. I won't be able to go to Sam's party this Friday night, . . .
16. I'm not afraid of flying, . . .
17. I haven't eaten breakfast yet, . . .
18. The other students weren't bored, . . .

Page 121 Exercise C
Listen and complete the sentences.

Ex. Nancy knows how to type, . . .
1. I'm interested in science, . . .
2. I won't be home this evening, . . .
3. I own my own business, . . .
4. I've never hooked up a computer, . . .
5. You just got a raise, . . .

Correlation Key

Student Text Pages	Activity Workbook Pages	Student Text Pages	Activity Workbook Pages
Chapter 1		**Chapter 7**	
2	2–3	82	78–79
3	4–5	84	80–81
4	6–8	86–87	82
7–8	9–11	88–89	83–84
		90–91	85–87
Chapter 2		**Chapter 8**	
12	12–13	96–97	88–89
13	14–17	100	90
14–15	18–19	101	91
18–19	20–23	104–105	92–93
		106–107	94–96
Chapter 3		109	97
22–23	24–26	**Check-Up Test**	**98–99**
25	27	**Chapter 9**	
26	28–29	116	100
27	30	117	101–102
28–29	31–33	119	103
Check-Up Test	**34–35**	122–123	104–105
Chapter 4		124	106–107
38	36	126–127	108
39	37	**Chapter 10**	
40	38	132	109–110
41	39	133	111–112
42–43	40–43	134–135	113
45	44–45	138–139	114–115
46	46–47	141	116–117
48	48–50	143	118–119
50	51	**Check-Up Test**	**120–121**
Chapter 5			
52–53	52–54		
56–57	55–57		
58–59	58–59		
62–63	60–61		
Chapter 6			
70–71	62–65		
72	66–68		
74–75	69–71		
76–77	72–75		
Check-Up Test	**76–77**		